MAJOR BUS OPERATORS

MANCHESTER AND MERSEYSIDE

Chester Transport
Halton Transport
Greater Manchester PTE
Merseyside PTE
National Travel (West)
Warrington Borough Council

DAVID KIRK

Capital Transport

First Published 1983

ISBN 0 904711 46 3

Published by Capital Transport Publishing
38 Long Elmes, Harrow Weald, Middlesex

Printed by SP Company (Westminster Press)
89 North Road, Brighton

Standard body codes are used throughout this publication, showing the body type, seating capacity and entrance position in that order.

Body Type	Single-deck bus	B
	Single-deck coach	C
	Convertible open-top double-deck bus	CO
	Double-deck coach	CH
	Dual-purpose vehicle	DP
	Highbridge double-deck bus	H
	Lowbridge double-deck bus	L
	Open-top single-deck bus	OB
	Open-top double-deck bus	O
	The further prefix 'F' is used for full-fronted vehicles where this is not normal for the type.	
Seating capacity	For double deckers the upper-deck capacity is shown first, followed by that for the lower deck. Standee capacities have not been shown as there are often local variations between the licensed capacity of a vehicle and the operational capacity agreed with road staff.	
Entrance Position	Separate entrance and exit (front and centre) with doors	D
	Front entrance with platform doors	F
	Rear entrance without doors	R
	Rear entrance with platform doors	RD

In the footnotes the letter w indicates a withdrawn vehicle

Acknowledgements
The author and publisher gratefully acknowledge the help given by the PSV Circle, the operating companies and Gordon Watts during the preparation of this book.

Contents

Cover Among the bus designs purchased for trials with Greater Manchester PTE is the Ailsa B55, three of which are in stock. The first of them, and the only one of the trio in the old livery, is No. 1446 delivered in 1980. It is seen at Stockport. *M.S. Stokes*

CHESTER CITY TRANSPORT

The origins of Chester City Transport can be traced back to a standard gauge horse tramway and horse buses operated by the Chester Tramways Company from 1879 to 1902. The tramway operation was taken over by Chester Corporation on 1st January 1902, the last horse car running in December 1902. The system was then converted to 3ft 6ins gauge and electric operation, the first of the reconstructed routes opening in April 1903.

The trams were replaced by buses during February 1930 and almost immediately new routes were opened up. An agreement was made with Crosville Motor Services in 1932 outlining the areas which were to be the responsibility of each operator. As a result, some services were transferred to Crosville, but the Corporation opened up new routes to the north west and south of the city. In the years since, the route network has been considerably expanded to take in new housing developments. Since local government reorganisation in 1974 removed constraints on its area of operation, more private hire work has been undertaken by Chester City Transport.

The original bus fleet comprised entirely of AECs and several further batches of this marque were purchased until 1940, together with Leylands between 1934 and 1941. There were also two Bedfords fitted for one-man operation which ran between 1934 and 1939. Seventeen Guys and Daimlers with utility bodywork were purchased between 1942 and 1945, not only as replacements, but to provide the additional resources to carry personnel to the military camps in the area. Between 1946 and 1948, Daimler double deckers and AEC single deckers were standard. From then until 1951 ten Foden double deckers were purchased, the choice of this relatively rare make being, no doubt, due to their manufacture in the County of Cheshire.

From 1953 to 1969 Guy Arabs were the standard double decker and the first example is still owned and licensed as a PSV some thirty years later. This is the last rear-entrance Arab still in local authority service. Indeed, Chester is the last local authority to operate Guy double deckers of any model. New single-deck requirements from 1966 have been met by Leyland Tiger Cubs and Leopards whilst from 1970 the Daimler (later Leyland) Fleetline was the standard double deck vehicle, being displaced from 1981 by the Dennis Dominator, which is the current standard. Massey Brothers supplied most bodies from 1934 until 1968. Since then, the principal supplier has been Northern Counties Motor & Engineering (NCME), the purchaser of the Massey business in 1967.

Livery is maroon and cream. The one exception is dual purpose single deck No. 80 which is in two shades of blue. The one garage is situated in Station Road.

Chester City Transport has retained its first Guy Arab IV of 1953 for thirty years. For some years it did duty as a trainer but has now returned to service on a restricted basis on special occasions. The distinctive rounded lines of Massey bodied No. 1 are shown in this view taken in 1969. G.R. Mills

A 1965 Guy Arab V with forward-entrance Massey bodywork of a squarer style has also been retained and No. 35 is seen here at Eccleston Village on an enthusiasts tour. R.L. Wilson

Typical of the first generation of Chester rear engined double deckers is No. 56, a Daimler Fleetline with Northern Counties body new in 1972. P.R. Gainsbury

Distinctive vehicles in the Chester fleet are three Northern Counties bodied Leyland Leopards delivered in 1976. No. 70 is seen in the city centre. D. Savage

No. 79 represents the batch of six Leyland Leopard PSU4s with Duple Dominant bodies purchased in 1976. This view shows the bus about to depart from the city centre. R.L. Wilson

Between 1977 and 1980 Leyland Fleetlines of the FE30AGR type with Northern Counties bodywork were the standard double decker, 18 being purchased. No. 92 of the 1979 delivery is seen at Northgate. D. Savage

Since 1981 eleven Dennis Dominators have been taken into stock. The last of the first batch, 103, is seen here when new, before the addition of the Chester City Transport insignia. The Northern Counties bodywork is similar to that on the Leyland Fleetlines. P.R. Gainsbury

CHESTER CITY TRANSPORT FLEET LIST

1 — **Chassis** Guy Arab IV 6LW; **Bodywork** Massey H30/26R; **Built** 1953; **Number in Stock** 1

1	RFM641

35 — **Chassis** Guy Arab V 6LW; **Bodywork** Massey H41/32F; **Built** 1965; **Number in Stock** 1

35	FFM135C

47 — **Chassis** Guy Arab V 6LW; **Bodywork** Northern Counties H41/32F; **Built** 1969; **Number in Stock** 1

47w	DFM347H

48–50

Chassis Daimler Fleetline CRG6LX
Bodywork Northern Counties H43/29F
Built 1970
Number in Stock 3

48 JFM648J **49** JFM649J **50** JFM650J

55–60

Chassis Daimler Fleetline CRG6LX
Bodywork Northern Counties H43/29F
Built Built 1972
Number in Stock 6

55 OFM955K **56** OFM956K **57** OFM957K **58** OFM958K **59** OFM959K **60** OFM960K

61–63

Chassis Daimler Fleetline CRG6LX
Bodywork Northern Counties H43/29F
Built 1974
Number in Stock 3

61 RFM61M **62** RFM62M **63** RFM63M

69–71

Chassis Leyland Leopard PSU4C/2R
Bodywork Northern Counties B43F
Built 1976
Number in Stock 3

69 NMB69P **70** NMB70P **71** NMB71P

75–80

Chassis Leyland Leopard PSU4D/2R
Bodywork Duple B47F (80: DP41F)
Built 1976
Number in Stock 6

75 TMB875R **76** TMB876R **77** TMB877R **78** TMB878R **79** TMB879R **80**a TMB880R

a In special private hire livery of two shades of blue.

81–83

Chassis Leyland Fleetline FE30AGR
Bodywork Northern Counties H43/29F
Built 1977
Number in Stock 3

81 VCA181R **82** VCA182R **83** VCA183R

84–88

Chassis Leyland Fleetline FE30AGR
Bodywork Northern Counties H43/29F
Built 1978
Number in Stock 5

84 CFM84S **85** CFM85S **86** CFM86S **87** CFM87S **88** CFM88S

89–93

Chassis Leyland Fleetline FE30AGR
Bodywork Northern Counties H43/29F
Built 1979
Number in Stock 5

89 KFM189T **90** KFM190T **91** KFM191T **92** KFM192T **93** KFM193T

94–98

Chassis Leyland Fleetline FE30AGR
Bodywork Northern Counties H43/29F
Built 1980
Number in Stock 5

94 SDM94V **95** SDM95V **96** SDM96V **97** SDM97V **98** SDM98V

99–103

Chassis Dennis Dominator DD121B
Bodywork Northern Counties H43/29F
Built 1981
Number in Stock 5

99 YMA99W **100** YMA100W **101** YMA101W **102** YMA102W **103** YMA103W

104–109

Chassis Dennis Dominator DDA150
Bodywork Northern Counties H43/29F
Built 1982
Number in Stock 6

104 HMA104X **105** HMA105X **106** HMA106X **107** KLG107Y **108** KLG108Y **109** KLG109Y

HALTON TRANSPORT

Until local government reorganisation in April 1974 the undertaking was operated by Widnes Corporation. The new borough of Halton incorporated a larger area including Runcorn, but services in this area continue to be operated by Crosville Motor Services and therefore Halton Transport's operations are still based on Widnes.

Most municipal operators started with tramways but Widnes was one of the few exceptions that commenced at an early stage with business (Commer double deckers). Operation started in 1909 after some trials using privately owned vehicles in 1907/8. Moreover, Widnes was certainly the first operator in England to use top-covered double deckers. All were rebuilt to single deck in 1917 and it was not until 1929 that double deckers were reintroduced.

The route network was considerably expanded and some services went well beyond the borough boundary due to the foresight of the Corporation in obtaining unrestricted operating powers in its enabling bill. From 1914 onwards Tilling Stevens petrol electrics were the standard bus, being purchased both new and second hand, the last one in 1929 being a double decker. In the 1930s most purchases were Leyland Lions and Titans with a small batch of conventional Tilling Stevens saloons and a pair of Crossley Condor double deckers. During the war Daimlers with utility bodies were purchased and by virtue of rebodying, some lasted more than twenty years. Following the war Leyland Titans and Royal Tigers were the mainstay of the fleet apart from the uncharacteristic purchase of four AEC Regent IIs from London Transport in 1955 (post-war STLs).

Since 1967 all new vehicles have been single deck, starting with Leyland Leopards, then Bristol REs and finally Leyland Nationals. Between 1969 and 1972 ten Leyland Titans were purchased second hand from Wigan Corporation but these have all been withdrawn, together with those bought new by Widnes, so that from 1980 no double deckers have been used in service.

The livery is cream and bright red, and buses are operated from a garage in the town centre in Moor Lane.

Halton No. 3 is an East Lancashire bodied Bristol RESL6L which entered service in 1973, preceded by similar vehicles 51-55 in 1971. It is seen in Widnes town centre which is the hub of Halton's operations. Apart from one training vehicle, the fleet is all single-deck. D. Savage

East Lancashire also bodied No. 6 which is on the longer Bristol RELL6L chassis. The shape of the front grille on the various batches of Bristols varies quite markedly. This view is at St Helens Town Hall at the end of one of the longer routes. R.L. Wilson

Until 1983 Leyland Leopard PSU3 No. 8, built in 1975, carried an unusual East Lancashire coach body. It was rebodied with a new East Lancashire bus body, together with sister vehicle 9, resembling the style of the 1971 batch of Bristols. D.D. Kirk

The 1975 batch of Bristol RELL6Ls have dual-purpose bodies by East Lancashire with yet another style of radiator grille. No. 11 is seen in Widnes town centre. D.D. Kirk

Halton has built up a large fleet of Leyland Nationals of various types. the 11351/2R with two doorways is represented by No. 15, built in 1976 and seen here in Runcorn near the site of the old Transporter Bridge. R.L. Wilson

A single door Leyland National 11351A/1R is seen here in Runcorn Old Town. No. 24 was built in 1979 and was the last mark 1 National bought by Halton. R.L. Wilson

Six Leyland National 2s of type NL116A are owned, the first five being 690 engined NL116AL11/1Rs. The newest vehicle, No. 30, however is of type NL116ATL11/1R with the turbocharged TL11 engine and is seen in Widnes shortly after delivery in 1983. D.D. Kirk

A most unusual addition to the fleet in 1982 was a secondhand 1975 Northern Counties bodied Leyland Leopard PSU4 from Chester City Transport, in which fleet it was numbered 68. Now Halton 18, it is seen approaching Widnes town centre. D.D. Kirk

HALTON TRANSPORT FLEET LIST

1

Chassis Leyland National 1151/1R/0101
Bodywork Leyland National B52F

Built 1972
Number in Stock 1

1 RTC645L

2–4

Chassis Bristol RESL6L
Bodywork East Lancs B42D

Built 1972/3
Number in Stock 3

2 TTB622L 3 TTB623L 4 TTB624L

5–7

Chassis Bristol RELL6L
Bodywork East Lancs B48D

Built 1973
Number in Stock 3

5 RTF305M 6 RTF306M 7 RTF307M

8/9

Chassis Leyland Leopard PSU3B/4R
Bodywork East Lancs B25F (new 1983)

Built 1975
Number in Stock 2

8 JFV294N 9 JFV295N

10–13

Chassis Bristol RELL6L
Bodywork East Lancs DP47D

Built 1975
Number in Stock 4

10 MCK210P 11 MCK211P 12 MCK212P 13 MCK213P

14–17

Chassis Leyland National 11351/2R
Bodywork Leyland National B48D

Built 1975/6
Number in Stock 4

14 OFR114P **15** OFR115P **16** OFR116P **17** OFR117P

18

Chassis Leyland Leopard PSU4/2R
Bodywork Northern Counties B47F
Acquired from Chester City Transport (68) in 1982

Built 1975
Number in Stock 1

18 HEN868N

19–21

Chassis Leyland National 11351A/2R
Bodywork Leyland National B48D

Built 1977
Number in Stock 3

19 ACW19R **20**a ACW20R **21** ACW21R

a Advertisement for Auto Centre

22–24

Chassis Leyland National 11351A/1R
Bodywork Leyland National B52F

Built 1979
Number in Stock 3

22 BTB22T **23** BTB23T **24** BTB24T

25–27

Chassis Leyland National 2 NL116AL11/1R
Bodywork Leyland National B52F

Built 1980
Number in Stock 3

25 HED203V **26** HED204V **27** HED205V

28/29

Chassis Leyland National 2 NL116AL11/1R
Bodywork Leyland National B52F

Built 1982
Number in Stock 2

28 CKC928X **29** CKC929X

30

Chassis Leyland National 2 NL116ATL11/1R
Bodywork Leyland National B52F

Built 1983
Number in Stock 1

30 EWM630Y

44–48

Chassis Leyland Leopard PSU4/1R
Bodywork East Lancs B42D

Built 1967/8
Number in Stock 2

44t FTB244F **48** KTB748F

t Training bus

49/50

Chassis Leyland Leopard PSU4A/2R
Bodywork East Lancs B42D

Built 1969
Number in Stock 2

49 STC149G **50**a STC150G

a In cream/light blue livery for courtesy service

51–55

Chassis Bristol RESL6L
Bodywork East Lancs B42D

Built 1971
Number in Stock 5

51 CTD51J **52** CTD52J **53** HTF353K **54** HTF354K **55** HTF355K

60

Chassis Leyland Titan PD2/12
Bodywork Leyland H33/28R
Acquired from Wigan Corporation (63) in 1970

Built 1953
Number in Stock 1

60t AEK505

t Training bus

GREATER MANCHESTER TRANSPORT

The Greater Manchester Passenger Transport Executive was set up on 1st April 1974 as part of the local government reorganisation which created the Greater Manchester Metropolitan County Council. It took over from the South East Lancashire and North East Cheshire Passenger Transport Executive (SELNEC) and additionally acquired Wigan Corporation's buses and services.

SELNEC itself had been formed on 1st November 1969 by taking over the operations of the corporations of Manchester, Salford, Leigh, Bolton, Bury, Rochdale, Oldham, Ashton-under-Lyne and Stockport together with the Stalybridge, Hyde, Mossley and Dukinfield Joint Board and Ramsbottom Urban District Council. It is interesting to note that with the exception of Bolton and with the addition of the North Western Road Car Company, these authorities had met in 1931 to discuss the setting up of a South East Lancashire and East Cheshire (SELEC) Passenger Transport Board; and so the new organisation put into effect an idea nearly forty years old.

It is not possible to give a detailed history of each constituent undertaking and only the main highlights of earlier developments can be given here. It was in 1824 that the first horse bus was placed in service by John Greenwood running in Manchester and Salford, and indeed it is claimed that this was the first bus service in Britain. Other proprietors came on the scene and in 1865 the Manchester Carriage Company was set up to consolidate these operations which also extended into Stockport.

Horse tramways started operation in May 1877, the tracks being constructed by the local authorities and leased to the Manchester Carriage Company to work. Plans had been drawn up by another operator, the Manchester Suburban Tramways company for services beyond the Manchester, Salford and Stockport boundaries and this company gained the lease in Oldham in 1878. In 1880, however, the two operating companies merged as the Manchester Carriage and Tramways Company, expanding the operation to Ashton-under-Lyne the following year. In 1880 horse trams came to Bolton (operated by Holden) and Wigan (operated by Wigan and District Tramways) although the Wigan system was converted to steam operation in 1883. The final horse tram operator, the Stockport and Hazel Grove Tramways Company commenced in 1889.

In the arc between the north and north east of the conurbation, steam trams on two gauges were introduced by the Manchester, Bury, Rochdale and Oldham Steam Tramways Limited in 1883, but despite the company's name it got no nearer to Manchester than Broughton, just in Salford. The system was later municipalised and this resulted in Heywood, a small town between Bury and Rochdale, running steam trams from 1904 to September 1905, thus becoming the last municipal steam tram operator in Britain. The Heywood operation was then taken over by Bury and Rochdale.

Towards the turn of the century more and more tramway systems throughout the country were being purchased by municipalities and electrified. On the first day of the new century Bolton Corporation ran the first municipally-owned electric tram of the constituent undertakings of the PTE. This was not however the first electric tramway in the areas as a BET subsidiary, the Oldham, Ashton and Hyde Tramways Company, had started a service in June 1899 which was to be subsequently purchased in 1921 by Ashton and the SHMD Board. A positive flurry of electrification then followed with Oldham later in 1900, Manchester, Salford and Stockport in 1901, Rochdale and Ashton in 1902, the SHMD Board, Bury and Wigan in 1903. It should be noted that Leigh and Ramsbottom never ran trams. Another small BET subsidiary was the Middleton Electric Traction Company whose operations and rolling stock were taken over by Manchester, Oldham and Rochdale in 1925.

The first municipal motorbuses started in Bolton in 1904, the only other additions in the Edwardian era being Manchester in 1906 and Stockport in 1908. It was not until the 1920s that the other municipalities commenced their own bus operations.

Meanwhile in 1913 Ramsbottom and Stockport commenced the operation of trolleybuses, the former using the conventional under-running double-wire overhead. Stockport, however, adopted the Lloyd-Kohler system which had the two wires vertically separated with a wheeled trolley running on the top wire and a small pantograph pressing on the lower wire. Only one set of wires was provided so that when vehicles passed in opposite directions they exchanged trolleys. Stockport abandoned its trolleybuses in 1919, whereas Ramsbottom kept its route going until 1931. The next trolleybus system was at Wigan where the remaining narrow gauge tram route was converted to trolleybuses in May 1925, although it was abandoned in favour of buses in October 1931.

In August 1925 Oldham and Ashton-under-Lyne converted the joint tram route between the two towns to trolleybus operation, but Oldham abandoned its operation precisely a year later in August 1926. Ashton persevered and continued operation of its portion of route until 1938, by which time there were developments elsewhere, and Ashton remained a trolleybus operator until 1966.

Towards the end of the 1920s, the motorbus became more reliable and some of the more lightly-used tramways were replaced by buses as the trams and track became worn out. With the advent of lower floors and top covers on double deckers the bus was becoming increasingly attractive and with the development of oil engines at the start of the thirties, operating costs were reduced even further. Thus even the more heavily-loaded trunk routes were being converted to buses and Wigan's last tram ran in March 1931 with Rochdale following in November 1932. With one exception, Ashton in 1938, the remaining systems survived the war, principally because it was policy during those years to conserve liquid fuel and rubber by making the most use of home produced electricity and steel.

The buses used on the conversions tended to be supplied by the local manufacturers in the form of Leyland Titans and Crossley Condors or Mancunians. Some Daimlers were also purchased by Oldham, Rochdale and the SHMD Board and right at the end of the thirties by Manchester. AEC Regents were represented in any numbers only at Salford and Rochdale. Towards the end of 1936 Manchester began introduction of its "streamliners" with curvaceous bodies and a paint style incorporating swoops and flashes in the relief colour. Several other operators in the area followed suit and the basic body style was to remain in production by Crossley into the early fifties.

A further municipal trolleybus operator in March 1936 was Bolton but the four vehicles involved were operated on its behalf by the South Lancashire Transport Company in whose livery the vehicles were also painted. It was not until 1958 when the Bolton-Leigh route was abandoned that these trolleybuses saw the inside of a Bolton garage, and then only whilst awaiting sale for scrap. In March 1938 a more far-reaching development was the introduction of modern trolleybuses in the "streamline" idiom by Manchester and Ashton-under-Lyne, which replaced the joint tram services between the two towns and on into SHMD territory to Stalybridge. The SHMD Board did not operate any trolleybuses itself, these were provided by Ashton and Manchester, but did erect the overhead. Many subsequent extensions were made to the trolleybus network until 1950. The last trolleybuses ran on 30th December 1966.

After the war the remaining tramways were abandoned. The SHMD Board's last ran in 1945 followed by Oldham in 1946 and Bolton and Salford in 1947. Bury and Manchester closed in 1949 leaving only Stockport which soldiered on until 1951.

A feature of the municipalities in the Greater Manchester area was the amount of joint operation which occurred. In the late twenties a network of jointly operated long distance express bus services had been built up with Manchester at the hub, but the routes ran across from one side to the other. However, the Traffic Commissioners set up by the 1930 Road Traffic Act did not approve of this form of operation and the routes had to be split in Manchester to the inconvenience of through passengers. With the total substitution of buses for trams, more joint through routes were introduced, although not on an express basis.

Vehicle policy after the war continued to be similar to the pre-war years except that Salford bought large numbers of Daimlers and a few Guys found their way into the Ashton fleet, whilst the SHMD Board bought some Leylands. In the rear-engined era the Leyland Atlantean was the most popular vehicle in the area, although Daimler Fleetlines were purchased in almost equal quantity by Manchester and exclusively by Rochdale and the SHMD Board with just a few going to Salford. Leigh ploughed a lonely furrough because of its need for low-height buses and purchased some Dennis Lolines and latterly quite a proportion of the fleet consisted of AEC Renowns. Indeed this fleet and those of Stockport and Ramsbottom contained no rear-engined double deckers when on 1st November 1969 SELNEC took over the operations of all the municipalities in the area apart from Wigan.

The varied liveries of the undertakings forming SELNEC were replaced by an orange and cream scheme and, although at first the new buses entering service were of orders placed previously, work started on the design of a standard bus. Some of the carried-over orders were modified so that the bodywork had elements of the new design built in. 1972 saw the introduction of the new generation of vehicles on a large scale with bodywork by Northern Counties on both Atlantean and Fleetline chassis. A smaller proportion of bodywork was built by Park Royal and although it resembled that builder's standard outline all the essential features of SELNEC's requirements were incorporated. At first some of the standard buses had two-door layouts, particularly those based in Manchester and Bolton, but eventually the single-door layout was adopted for all vehicles.

On 4th March 1972 that part of the operations of the North Western Road Car Company which was within the SELNEC area was acquired. This was achieved by the purchase of the shares of the North Western (SELNEC Division) Road Car Company, a company formed in November 1971 to take over, on 1st January 1972, North Western's stage activities in the SELNEC area. North Western dated from 1923, when it took over the operations of the British Automobile Traction Company in the Macclesfield area. Services were developed over much of East Cheshire including many running into Manchester and Stockport. Latterly many of the services were joint with SELNEC. As a result of this purchase many different varieties joined the SELNEC fleet including Leyland Tiger Cubs and Leopards, AEC Reliances and Bristol RE single deckers with Dennis Loline, AEC Renown and Daimler Fleetline double deckers. North Western Road Car continued in existence as an express operator but was later renamed National Travel (North West).

With local government reorganisation, SELNEC became the Greater Manchester Passenger Transport Executive on 1st April 1974 and took over Wigan Corporation's operations at that time. In the near decade that has now elapsed services have been extensively revised and the vehicles acquired from the constituent undertakings have to a large extent been replaced by "Standards" or Leyland Nationals.

Greater Manchester PTE has developed a coaching business based initially on the activities of SELNEC (largely inherited from Manchester Corporation), but later by acquisition of operators in the coaching field. The first was Warburton's of Bury in November 1975, no vehicles being acquired. The PTE's own operations were renamed Charterplan in 1976 and moved to a separate base at the ex North Western Charles Street, Stockport garage. In November of that year Godfrey Abbott of Sale was acquired with twenty-one vehicles. Amongst the licences was one for a regular Manchester-Birmingham-Paris service, the only international operation by a Passenger Transport Executive. Also taken over with the business were nine small vehicles jointly owned by the PTE and used on a "Dial a Ride" service which henceforth became a separate operating unit until February 1981 when merged into the main Greater Manchester fleet. Although all coaches are licensed to the PTE they still carry Warburton's, Charterplan, Godfrey Abbott and Lancashire United fleetnames and the services are independently marketed.

On 1st January 1976 the PTE acquired the old established Lancashire United Transport Company, until then the largest independent operator in the country. It continued to operate as a separate entity with its own livery for the next five years.

On 1st April 1981 Lancashire United was absorbed into the main Greater Manchester fleet. LUT had its origins in the South Lancashire Tramways undertaking which operated a network of lines based upon Atherton stretching to St Helens, Bolton, Leigh and Farnworth, the first car running in October 1902. From July 1930 the system was progressively converted to trolleybus operation, the last tram running in December 1933. The trolleybuses were themselves replaced by buses between 1956 and 1958, the last one running on 31st August. Remarkably some of the original vehicles were still running at the end. The replacing buses were operated by Lancashire United. Apart from the buses used on the 1956 conversions, SLT had never operated motor buses. Lancashire United had itself started bus services, its first two attempts being short lived in 1906 and 1914. From 1919 however bus services were developed over a wide area of South Lancashire, many being jointly operated with other companies and municipalities. As with the trolleybuses Atherton was the hub of the system. Vehicle policy was very individualistic, and in the post-war era although the Guy Arab was the mainstay of the fleet, almost all of the heavyweight chassis makes were to be found including relatively rare Fodens, Dennises and Atkinsons. The fleet which passed to Greater Manchester included Seddons, Bristols, Daimler Fleetlines, Leyland Leopards, Leyland Nationals and Volvo B58 coaches as well as the last few surviving Guy Arabs.

The PTE livery is orange and white with a brown skirt, and Charterplan coaches are white with orange and brown stripes. The Godfrey Abbott, Lancashire United and Warburton coaches have distinctive liveries of white with different coloured stripes; viz lime green/olive green, red/yellow and duo-tone blue respectively. Several coaches for use on service 200 (Manchester Airport) are painted blue, white and orange.

Garages are situated at Altrincham, Atherton, Bolton, Bury, Glossop, Hindley, Leigh, Manchester (Birchfields Road, Hyde Road, Northendon, Princess Road and Queens Road), Oldham, Ramsbottom, Rochdale, Salford (Frederick Road and Weaste), Stockport (Daw Bank and Charles Street), Swinton, Tameside and Wigan.

Greater Manchester PTE's Eastern Coachworks bodied Leyland Leopard PSU3 coaches are now being increasingly used on normal bus duties and No. 56 of 1973 is depicted on such work at Stockport. D.D. Kirk

Greater Manchester PTE purchased 85 of the shorter 10351/1R type Leyland National in 1975 and 1977, and these were followed by a batch of 20 of the longer version. No. 136 of the 1975 delivery is seen in the new livery with brown skirt. Capital Transport

Typical of the Leyland Nationals of type 11351A/1R acquired from Lancashire United is 225, new in 1978 and seen on a crew operated duty at Warrington. D. Savage

Some of the Nationals inherited from Lancashire United have not yet been repainted into GMT colours. Red liveried No. 224 is also seen at Warrington. D. Savage

The need for shorter vehicles with a reasonable capacity on the route to Holcombe Brook has resulted in the retention in the operational fleet of three ex-North Western Road Car Company Bristol RESL6Gs at Bury. They have Marshall bodies of BET design and were built in 1969. No. 299 is seen at Bury. M.S. Stokes

In all-orange livery and carrying the Lancashire United Transport fleetname is 418, a 1974 Bristol RESL6G with Plaxton dual-purpose body seen at Swinton garage. R.L. Wilson

Also seen at Swinton garage is 424, a unique 1974 Leyland Leopard PSU3 with Northern Counties dual-purpose body. This vehicle has however acquired a Greater Manchester fleetname. R.L. Wilson

A large number of Leyland Leopard PSU3s with Plaxton bus bodies were placed in service by LUT in 1976. No. 440 is seen in Warrington in 1983, still in red and grey livery but with fleetname and insignia deleted, while No. 446 is seen in the latest livery at St Helens on the one-time South Lancs/St Helens trolleybus service.
D.D. Kirk/D. Savage

Manchester's 'Mancunians' were among the first one-man double deckers in the country, the initial batch entering service shortly after the Transport Act of 1968, which permitted double-deck omo, became law. The first batch of Mancunians was based on the Atlantean PDR1 chassis and only one of these remained in service at the time this book was compiled, No. 1024. The batch which followed was built on the longer PDR2 chassis and during 1969 an unrepeated order for single-door Mancunians entered service, of which No. 1135 is seen in Bury. Bodywork on most of the Mancunians with Atlantean chassis was by Park Royal, but East Lancashire also built some, including all of the single-door examples. Only a few of this batch remain in use. M.R. Keeley

East Lancashire also built some dual doorway bodied PDR2s in 1969 and four of these remain in service at the time of writing, although 1145 seen in Portland Street, Manchester was withdrawn in 1982. R.L. Wilson

A batch of twenty Leyland Atlantean PDR2s with Park Royal bodies had been ordered by Salford Corporation and SELNEC was able to change the specification to be broadly similar to the Mancunian design. However, standard Salford destination equipment was fitted, as shown by No. 1214 of 1970 at Victoria Bus Station. This bus was withdrawn in 1982 but remains in stock.
R.L. Wilson

Below **One of the first production Leyland Nationals (type 1151/2R/0202) swings into Chapel Street, Salford. No. 1332 was built in 1972 and together with the shorter Nationals of 1973 are the only examples with two doors in the Greater Manchester fleet.** Bottom **No. 1339 is an example of the 1973 delivery of Leyland Nationals of the short 1051/2R/2804 type and is seen in the orange and white livery at Eccles Bus Station.**
M.S. Stokes/R.L. Wilson

Photographed in Leigh Station is 1349, a Scania BR111MH of 1972. These Metro-Cammell Weymann bodied vehicles are of 11-metre nominal length with dual doorways. M.R. Keeley

Also seen at Leigh Bus Station is No. 1351 of Scania type BR110MH, built a year later in 1973. The four vehicles in this batch have shorter 10-metre Metro-Cammell Weymann bodies, seating four fewer at 40. M.R. Keeley

North Western Road Car Company had on order twenty five Eastern Coachworks bodied Bristol VRTs at the time of acquisition and these were delivered direct to SELNEC in 1973. No. 1417 was photographed at Stockport Bus Station in the orange and white livery, but many of the batch are now in the new brown skirted scheme. B.J. Hemming

Four Dennis Dominators with Northern Counties bodywork have been taken into Greater Manchester stock for evaluation purposes. One of the first pair, 1437, is seen at Piccadilly. D. Savage

No. 1446 is a 1980 Volvo Ailsa B55-10 with Northern Counties body based at Stockport for evaluation purposes. The bodywork has a standard Volvo grille and the glazing of the side windows is slightly recessed. M.R. Keeley

In 1982 a further two Volvo Ailsa B55-10s were purchased, again with Northern Counties bodies, but this time of virtually standard mark 1A form. However 1447 seen in Wigan shows the revised frontal treatment. L.J. Bowles

An early example of the Bristol built Leyland Olympian with Northern Counties bodywork was taken into stock for evaluation in 1980 and subsequently 25 of this combination were ordered. No. 1451 is seen at Oldham. M.S. Stokes

Left **No. 3007 of the batch of 25 Olympians is seen climbing Dan Bank into Marple in April 1983 shortly after entering service.** Right **Further vehicles bought for evaluation are two Scania BR112DH buses with Northern Counties bodywork. The first of these is seen in late-March 1983 at Charles Street works, Stockport prior to entering service. The body design appears to follow the mark 1A version of the Standard body rather than the current light alloy type.** M.S. Stokes.

One of the first sights to be seen by the visitor arriving at Manchester (Piccadilly) Station is a line-up of Seddon IV midibuses on the station approach road. No. 1721 of 1974 heads a line of three, all with Seddon bodies, on the Centreline service to Victoria Station. The fare is currently twelve pence. M.R. Keeley

More Mancunians were built on Daimler Fleetline chassis than on Leyland Atlanteans and therefore many more of them remain in service. Currently the oldest in use on passenger duties is 2108 seen in Aytoun Street, Manchester. It has a CRG6LXB-33 chassis with Park Royal body and was new in 1970. D.D. Kirk

The next batch of Mancunians with CRG6LXB-33 chassis was delivered in 1970/1 with Metro-Cammell Weymann bodies. No. 2209 is about to be overtaken by Northern Counties bodied Fleetline No. 7314 in the new livery. Capital Transport

The last batch of Mancunians was delivered in 1972 and are all still in service at the time of writing. Based as usual on Daimler Fleetline CRG6LXB-33 chassis, the bodywork is by Roe but is virtually identical to the 1971 Park Royal delivery. 2271 is seen in Piccadilly, Manchester less than half way through its journey on the long route from Chorlton cum Hardy to Waterhead. M.R. Keeley

Twenty DMS class Daimler Fleetlines were acquired from London Transport in 1980 by LUT and passed to Greater Manchester Transport in 1981. No. 2331, seen at Greengate, Salford, is a 1973 CRL6 with Leyland 0680 engine and Park Royal bodywork rebuilt to single-door layout. It had been London Transport DMS710. In the photograph the vehicle is still carrying the Lancashire United Transport fleetname and its LUT number. The livery is the standard one applied to LUT double deckers from 1980 onwards, being orange with the between-decks panels in white. M.R. Keeley

A batch of single-door and dual-door Northern Counties bodied Fleetlines joined the GMT fleet when Lancashire United was absorbed. No. 2398 was photographed in September 1982. Capital Transport

Six of the 1971 Leyland Atlantean PDR2s with Northern Counties dual-doorway bodies acquired from Wigan Corporation remain in public service. Formerly Wigan 94, No. 3312 is numerically the oldest and is seen in Market Street, Wigan on short local route 626. D.D. Kirk

All of the 1972 Northern Counties dual-doorway bodied Leyland Atlantean AN68/2Rs taken over from Wigan Corporation are still in service and many like 3332, seen in Wigan, have received the new livery. The change to flat windscreens produces a complete change in the look of the bus. The lights on each side of the route number display were a typical Wigan feature and were lit green at night to distinguish Corporation buses from LUT or Ribble buses. Presumably due to Greater Manchester PTE's statutory duty to integrate services there is no longer a need to advertise the local municipal service and the lights have been painted out. L.J. Bowles

Between 1978 and 1980, fifteen Leyland Titan TNs were purchased for evaluation. Five were of the TNTL11RF type with TL11 Leyland engines, whilst the remainder were of the Gardner 6LXB engined TNLXB1RF type. 4002 is one of the Gardner engined vehicles, new in 1978. D. Savage

Following an evaluation batch of ten DR101 type MCW Metrobuses in 1979, a further 180 Metrobuses were ordered, all of type DR102 with Gardner 6LXB engines, air brakes and Metro-Cammell Weymann mark 1 bodies. So far 160 of this order have been delivered and No. 5117 at Glossop shows the livery which most carry, being of the same style as that applied to LUT double deckers. L.J. Bowles

Amongst the vehicles ordered by constituent undertakings but delivered direct to SELNEC were twelve East Lancashire dual doorway bodied Leyland Atlantean PDR1As outstanding for Oldham Corporation. Six remain in public service and 5191, new in 1971, is seen passing the Oldham offices of that well known independent, Yelloway. The peak dome was a feature of both Oldham Corporation and East Lancashire. M.S. Stokes

Several outstanding orders of the constituents were changed by SELNEC to develop the Standard body design. Amongst these were a batch of six vehicles ordered by Ashton Corporation which entered service in 1971 as EX1-6. They have Leyland Atlantean PDR1A chassis and Northern Counties bodies and clearly form the basis of the mark 1 Standard. No. 5471 was originally EX6. G.W. Potter

Greater Manchester have continued to use their older buses for driver training purposes, in some cases for many years after withdrawal from public service. Hence it was possible in March 1983 to photograph 5832, a 1964 Leyland Titan PD2/40 with East Lancashire bodywork which had been withdrawn from passenger duties in 1979. These training buses roam far and wide, this one (originally Stockport 32) being seen in Blackhorse Street, Bolton. D.D. Kirk

Another order modified to develop the Standard body was one originally placed by Rochdale Corporation but delivered to SELNEC in 1972. The batch consisted of five Daimler Fleetline CRG6LXBs with Northern Counties single doorway bodies and five with dual doorways. No. 6253 is seen leaving Rochdale for the Wardle terminus of the horseshoe shaped 447 route. R.L. Wilson

An order placed by Bury Corporation for Daimler Fleetline CRG6LXs with East Lancashire dual-doorway bodywork was delivered to SELNEC in 1970/1. The typical peaked dome style is well illustrated by 6349, parked in the reserve bus area at Bury bus/rail interchange. M.S. Stokes

The final inherited order still in public service today is a batch of fifteen Leyland Atlantean PDR2s with East Lancashire bodies, which had been specified by Bolton Corporation. They were delivered in 1971/2 incorporating SELNEC standard destination displays and all are still in service. Some have recently been repainted in the new livery. The buses have a single doorway and because of their length, can accommodate 86 seated passengers. No. 6816 dates from 1972. Capital Transport

Lancashire United Transport was supplied with ninety Leyland Fleetlines of the FE30 type with Gardner 6LXB engines and Northern Counties bodies to the Greater Manchester mark 1A Standard design between 1977 and 1980. This was because LUT was a wholly-owned subsidiary of the PTE during this period. One of the 1980 vehicles is 6989. Capital Transport

With the formation of SELNEC PTE a large number of types of vehicle to each individual operator's specification was inherited. The PTE decided that it would be advantageous to develop a "Standard" bus for its future requirements. Accordingly some of the orders which had been placed by constituent undertakings were modified in specification to develop the design. It was also intended, however, to obtain both bodies and chassis on a dual sourcing basis from Northern Counties and Park Royal, in the case of the former, and, Daimler Fleetline and Leyland Atlantean for the latter. Ironically production of the Fleetline was transferred from Coventry to Leyland in 1973 and in the event all later chassis were built at the same place. The first Standards went into service in 1972 and the Northern Counties batch included dual-doorway examples for service in Manchester and Rochdale. Only 48 of the latter were built in 1972/3 and thereafter the single doorway design was the only one specified. In the pictorial review which follows, Park Royal bodies are illustrated first and then the rather larger number of Northern Counties vehicles.

PARK ROYAL STANDARDS

The mark 1 version is most easily identifiable by the flat windscreens. Leyland Atlantean AN68 No. 7039 was delivered in 1972 and is seen in Piccadilly, Manchester about to turn into Portland Street. It is still in the original orange and white livery. D.D. Kirk

One of the 1972 Leyland Atlantean AN68s with a Park Royal mark 1 Standard body was damaged in a low bridge accident and was converted to open top in 1982. No. 7032 is seen at Stockport garage, which traditionally houses a PTE open topper. R.L. Wilson

Park Royal mark 1 Standard bodies were also mounted on Daimler Fleetline CRG6LXB chassis and No. 7175 of 1973 is seen in Bolton. Capital Transport

The mark 1A body differs principally in having curved windscreens. All Park Royal built bodies to this design were mounted on Leyland Atlantean AN68 chassis including 7896. Capital Transport

NORTHERN COUNTIES STANDARDS

Forty-eight of the Northern Counties mark 1 Standards were of dual-doorway configuration, all being on Daimler Fleetline CRG6LXB chassis. Seen in the latest livery is No. 7229. Capital Transport

The curved windscreens identify 7487 as a mark 1A Standard, but another significant variation from 7229 is the Fleetline CRG6LXB chassis built at Leyland. This vehicle dates from 1976 and is seen at Bolton. Capital Transport

A further 150 of the mark 1A Standards were built by Northern Counties on the revised Leyland Fleetline FE30GR chassis. Many of Greater Manchester's routes are hilly and this is well illustrated in this view of 8048 coming into Rawtenstall. The bus was new in 1979. R.L. Wilson

Production of the Northern Counties mark 1A Standard totalled 559 on Leyland Atlantean AN68 chassis against 256 on both types of Fleetline. The Leyland based combination is represented by 1981 delivery 8379. Capital Transport

The latest version of the Northern Counties Standard has light alloy framing and this has resulted in some differences in appearance. Principal identifying features are the reversion to a centre pillar in the front upper deck windows and recessed glazing all round rather than the flush mounted type favoured hitherto. Capital Transport

Atlantean 8521 is seen at Piccadilly Gardens Bus Station in Manchester in all-over advertising livery for car dealers, Lookers. The vehicle behind is a similar Atlantean with light alloy Standard body, 8585, in all over livery for the Bus and Coach Council. Unusually both were in service on route 266, it being a relatively rare occurrence for two all over advertising buses to be on consecutive runnings. Both were new in 1982 but 8521 has an AN68B/1R chassis whilst 8585 has an AN68D/1R chassis. D.D. Kirk

Above **Greater Manchester's Godfrey Abbott fleet contains five Duple bodied AEC Reliances with ZF gearboxes. No. 7 is seen in the now superseded upswept stripe livery.** R.L. Wilson

Upper left **Seen in the coach park at Birmingham's National Exhibition Centre on a trip to the 1982 Motor Show is Charterplan's 21, a Leyland Tiger with Duple Dominant body. Like 7 it has a ZF gearbox, as standard on most recent deliveries to Greater Manchester's coaching unit. No. 21 is in the recently revised livery using horizontal stripes.** M.G. Norton

Lower left **Manchester United's team coach is Godfrey Abbott No. 26, a Leyland Leopard PSU5 with Duple Dominant body seating only 32 and equipped with a toilet.** R.L. Wilson

The most recent additions to the Charterplan fleet are of great interest in being of German manufacture and with 'cherished' registration marks. No. 31 is a Kassbohrer Setra S215HD delivered this year and has a rear mounted Mercedes Benz engine driving through a ZF gearbox. The use of cherished registration marks on expensive coaches is becoming relatively common so that their year of manufacture is not so obvious and the investment can be spread over a longer period. The registration number 583TD was formerly carried by ex-Lancashire United Transport Guy Arab IV TV5 which has been re-registered BNC989B. There is a variation in the livery of the two Setras with the main background colour below the windows being a silvery grey. No. 31 was photographed on the Charterplan stand at Stockport Bus Station, having just set down a party of farmers returning from an agricultural show in Paris. D.D. Kirk

Resplendent in the Lancashire United livery is Volvo B58/Plaxton Supreme 49, one of three purchased in 1980. R.L. Wilson

Older luxury coaches are cascaded down from longer-distance duties to operate the Manchester Airport express service, where their luggage boots are useful. One such vehicle is No. 70, a 1973 Leyland Leopard PSU3 with Plaxton body seen here in Cannon Street, Manchester. A special livery is used with a broad blue band beneath the windows, in addition to the white, orange and brown house colours. D.D. Kirk

In 1981/2 seven Leyland Leopard PSU3s, with Eastern Coachworks bodies, similar to No. 62 but dating from 1975, were rebuilt and rebodied with new Duple Dominant coachwork. They were also re-registered and the resulting combination is illustrated by No. 86 photographed in the new Charterplan livery. D. Savage

GREATER MANCHESTER TRANSPORT FLEET LIST

1/2

Chassis Leyland Leopard PSU5C/4R
Bodywork Duple C55F(1), C48F(2)

Built 1978
Number in Stock 2

1c ANA1T	2c ANA2T

c Charterplan livery

3/4

Chassis Leyland Leopard PSU3E/4R
Bodywork Duple C44F(3), C51F(4)

Built 1978
Number in Stock 2

3c ANA3T	4b ANA4T

b Warburton livery   c Charterplan livery

5–9

Chassis AEC Reliance 6U3ZR
Bodywork Plaxton C53F

Built 1978
Number in Stock 5

5a ANA5T	**6**a ANA6T	**7**a ANA7T	**8**a ANA8T	**9**a ANA9T

a Godfrey Abbott livery

18

Chassis AEC Reliance 6U3ZR
Bodywork Plaxton C44FT

Built 1977
Number in Stock 1

18a RVU539R

a Godfrey Abbott livery

21–24

Built Leyland Tiger TRCTL11/3R
Bodywork Duple C46F

Built 1982/3
Number in Stock 4

21c BJA856Y	**22**c FWH22Y	**23**c FWH23Y	**24**c FWH24Y

c Charterplan livery

26/27

Chassis Leyland Leopard PSU5D/4R
Bodywork Duple C32FT(26), C42F(27)

Built 1980
Number in Stock 2

26am MNC500W	**27**b MNC501W

a Godfrey Abbott livery b Warburton livery m Manchester United team coach

28/29

Chassis Leyland Leopard PSU3E/4R
Bodywork Duple C44F

Built 1980
Number in Stock 2

28c MNC502W	**29**c MNC503W

c Charterplan livery

30/1

Chassis Kassbohrer 5215HD
Bodywork Kassbohrer C49FT

Built 1983
Number in Stock 2

30c 515VTB	**31**c 583TD

c Charterplan livery

33–48

Chassis Leyland Leopard PSU3E/4R
Bodywork Plaxton C51F
Acquired from Lancashire United 480-4, 537-41, 566-9 in 1981

Built 1977-9
Number in Stock 14

35e OTD824R	**38**e OTD827R	**41**d TWH686T	**44**d TWH689T	**47**d YBN631V
36e OTD825R	**39**b OTD828R	**42**d TWH687T	**45**d YBN629V	**48**d YBN632V
37e OTD826R	**40**d TWH685T	**43**d TWH688T	**46**d YBN630V	

b Warburton livery d Lancashire United livery e Manchester Airport express livery

49–51

Chassis Volvo B58-61
Bodywork Plaxton C55F
Acquired from Lancashire United 614-6 in 1981

Built 1980
Number in Stock 3

49d DEN245W	**50**d DEN246W	**51**d DEN247W

d Lancashire United livery

56–64

Chassis Leyland Leopard PSU3B/4R
Bodywork Eastern Coachworks C47F

Built 1973
Number in Stock 10

56	AJA357L	**58**	AJA359L	**60**	AJA361L	**62**	AWH62L	**64**	AWH64L
57	AJA358L	**59**w	AJA360L	**61**	AJA362L	**63**	AWH63L	**65**w	AWH65L

70–75

Chassis Leyland Leopard PSU3B/4R
Bodywork Plaxton C49F

Built 1973
Number in Stock 6

70e	XNE882L	**72**e	XNE884L	**73**w	XNE885L	**74**w	XNE886L	**75**	XNE887L
71e	XNE883L								

e Manchester Airport express livery

77/78

Chassis Leyland Leopard PSU5A/4R
Bodywork Duple C51F

Built 1974
Number in Stock 2

77c	YNA398M	**78**c	YNA399M

c Charterplan livery

80/81

Chassis Leyland Leopard PSU3B/4R
Bodywork Eastern Coachworks C49F

Built 1975
Number in Stock 2

80	HNE640N	**81**	HNE641N

82–88

Chassis Leyland Leopard PSU3B/4R rebuilt
Bodywork Duple C51F
Rebuilt from 1975 chassis

Built 1981/2
Number in Stock 7

82c	SND82X	**84**b	SND84X	**86**a	SND86X	**87**a	SND87X	**88**a	SND88X
83c	SND83X	**85**b	SND85X						

a Godfrey Abbott livery b Warburton livery c Charterplan livery

90/91

Chassis Leyland Leopard PSU3C/4R
Bodywork Eastern Coachworks C49F

Built 1975
Number in Stock 2

90	KDB677P	**91**	KDB678P

97

Chassis Leyland Leopard PSU5A/4R
Bodywork Duple C55F

Built 1975
Number in Stock 1

97t	JND997N

t Training bus

101–185

Chassis Leyland National 10351/1R
Bodywork Leyland National B41F

Built 1975/77
Number in Stock 84

101	HNB20N	**118**	HNE648N	**135**	JNA591N	**152**	KBU889P	**170**	KBU905P
102	HNB21N	**119**	HNE649N	**136**	JNA592N	**153**	KBU890P	**171**	RBU171R
103	HNB22N	**120**	HNE650N	**137**	JNA593N	**154**	KBU891P	**172**	RBU172R
104	HNB23N	**121**	HNE651N	**138**	JNA594N	**155**	KBU892P	**173**	RBU173R
105	HNB24N	**122**	HNE652N	**139**	JNA595N	**156**	JVM980N	**174**	RBU174R
106	HNB46N	**123**	HJA127N	**140**	JNA596N	**157**	JVM981N	**175**	RBU175R
107	HNB47N	**124**	HJA128N	**141**	JNA597N	**158**	KBU893P	**176**	RBU176R
108	HNB48N	**125**	HJA129N	**142**	JNA598N	**159**	KBU894P	**177**	RBU177R
109	HNE633N	**126**	HJA130N	**143**	JNA599N	**160**	KBU895P	**178**	RBU178R
110	HNE634N	**127**	HJA131N	**144**	JNA600N	**161**	KBU896P	**179**	RBU179R
111	HNE635N	**128**	JNA584N	**145**	JNA601N	**162**	KBU897P	**180**	RBU180R
112	HNE636N	**129**	JNA585N	**146**	JNA602N	**163**	KBU898P	**181**	RBU181R
113	HNE637N	**130**	JNA586N	**147**	JNA603N	**164**	KBU899P	**182**	RBU182R
114	HNE638N	**131**	JNA587N	**148**	JND991N	**165**	KBU900P	**183**	RBU183R
115	HNE639N	**132**	JNA588N	**149**	JND998N	**166**	KBU901P	**184**	RBU184R
116	HNE646N	**133**	JNA589N	**150**	JND999N	**167**	KBU902P	**185**	RBU185R
117	HNE647N	**134**	JNA590N	**151**	JDB103N	**169**	KBU904P		

186–250

Chassis Leyland National 11351A/1R
Bodywork Leyland National B49F
206-50 Acquired from Lancashire United (465-79, 530-6, 543-65) in 1981

Built 1977-9
Number in Stock 65

186	ABA11T	**199**	ABA24T	**212**	NEN958R	**225**	PTD671S	**238**	WBN472T
187	ABA12T	**200**	ABA25T	**213**	NEN959R	**226**	PTD672S	**239**	WBN473T
188	ABA13T	**201**	ABA26T	**214**	NEN960R	**227**	PTD673S	**240**	WBN474T
189	ABA14T	**202**	ABA27T	**215**	NEN961R	**228**	WBN462T	**241**	WBN475T
190	ABA15T	**203**	ABA28T	**216**	NEN962R	**229**	WBN463T	**242**	WBN476T
191	ABA16T	**204**	ABA29T	**217**	NEN963R	**230**	WBN464T	**243**	WBN477T
192	ABA17T	**205**	ABA30T	**218**	NEN964R	**231**	WBN465T	**244**	WBN478T
193	ABA18T	**206**	NEN952R	**219**	NEN965R	**232**	WBN466T	**245**	WBN479T
194	ABA19T	**207**	NEN953R	**220**	NEN966R	**233**	WBN467T	**246**	WBN480T
195	ABA20T	**208**	NEN954R	**221**	PTD667S	**234**	WBN468T	**247**	WBN481T
196	ABA21T	**209**	NEN955R	**222**	PTD668S	**235**	WBN469T	**248**	WBN482T
197	ABA22T	**210**	NEN956R	**223**	PTD669S	**236**	WBN470T	**249**	WBN483T
198	ABA23T	**211**	NEN957R	**224**	PTD670S	**237**	WBN471T	**250**	WBN484T

291–301

Chassis Bristol RESL6G
Bodywork Marshall B43F
Acquired from North Western (same numbers) in 1972

Built 1968
Number in Stock 4

291	KJA291G	**299**	KJA299G	**300**w	KJA300G	**301**	KJA301G

317–344

Chassis Bristol RELL6G
Bodywork Alexander B48F
Acquired from North Western (same numbers) in 1972

Built 1969
Number in Stock 8

317w	NJA317H	**324**w	NJA324H	**337**w	NJA337H	**340**w	NJA340H	**343**w	NJA343H
319w	NJA319H	**325**w	NJA325H	**338**w	NJA338H				

347–393

Chassis Seddon RU
Bodywork Plaxton B40D
Acquired from Lancashire United (338/50/2-4/64/6/9-70/184/92) in 1981

Built 1970/1
Number in Stock 13

347w	WTD671H	**353**w	WTD686H	**366**w	DTC714J	**371**w	DTC719J	**384**w	DTC732J
350w	WTD683H	**354**w	WTD687H	**369**w	DTC717J	**379**w	DTC727J	**392**w	DTC740J
352w	WTD685H	**364**w	DTC712J	**370**w	DTC718J				

414–423

Chassis Bristol RESL6G
Bodywork Plaxton DP41F
Acquired from Lancashire United (Same numbers) in 1981

Built 1974
Number in Stock 10

414	TTB445M	**416**	TTB447M	**418**	TTB449M	**420**	TTB451M	**422**	TTB453M
415	TTB446M	**417**	TTB448M	**419**	VTC733M	**421**	TTB452M	**423**	TTB454M

424

Chassis Leyland Leopard PSU3B/2R
Bodywork Northern Counties DP44F
Acquired from Lancashire United (424) in 1981

Built 1974
Number in Stock 1

424	GBN331N

430/431

Chassis Leyland Leopard PSU3C/4R
Bodywork Plaxton B48D
Acquired from Lancashire United (430/1) in 1981

Built 1975
Number in Stock 2

430	JDK921P	**431**	JDK922P

432–434

Chassis Leyland Leopard PSU4C/4R
Bodywork Plaxton B44F
Acquired from Lancashire United (432-4) in 1981

Built 1975
Number in Stock 3

432	JDK923P	**433**	JDK924P	**434**	JDK925P

435–464

Chassis Leyland Leopard PSU3C/4R
Bodywork Plaxton B48F
Acquired from Lancashire United (same numbers) in 1981

Built 1976
Number in Stock 30

435	LTE486P	**441**	LTE492P	**447**	MTE15R	**453**	MTE21R	**459**	MTE27R
436	LTE487P	**442**	LTE493P	**448**	MTE16R	**454**	MTE22R	**460**	MTE28R
437	LTE488P	**443**	LTE494P	**449**	MTE17R	**455**	MTE23R	**461**	MTE29R
438	LTE489P	**444**	LTE495P	**450**	MTE18R	**456**	MTE24R	**462**	MTE30R
439	LTE490P	**445**	MTE13R	**451**	MTE19R	**457**	MTE25R	**463**	MTE31R
440	LTE491P	**446**	MTE14R	**452**	MTE20R	**458**	MTE26R	**464**	MTE32R

1024

Chassis Leyland Atlantean PDR1/1
Bodywork Park Royal H45/28D
Acquired from Manchester Corporation (1024) in 1969

Built 1968
Number in Stock 1

1024 HVM924F

1079–1219

Chassis Leyland Atlantean PDR2/1
Park Royal H47/29D (1079-1126)
East Lancs H47/32F (1132-42)
East Lancs H47/26D (1143-51)
Park Royal H47/28D (1161-92)
Park Royal H47/30D (1202-19)
1079-87 Acquired from Manchester Corporation (same numbers) in 1969

Built 1968-70
Number in Stock 89

1079w	LNA179G	**1112**w	NNB521H	**1139**w	NNB544H	**1170**	ONF858H	**1189**	ONF877H
1080t	LNA180G	**1113**	NNB522H	**1142**	NNB547H	**1171**	ONF859H	**1190**	ONF878H
1081w	LNA181G	**1115**	NNB524H	**1143**w	NNB548H	**1172**	ONF860H	**1191**	ONF879H
1086w	LNA186G	**1117**w	NNB526H	**1144**	NNB549H	**1173**	ONF861H	**1192**	ONF880H
1089t	LNA189G	**1118**w	NNB527H	**1146**	NNB551H	**1174**	ONF862H	**1202**t	SRJ325H
1090t	LNA190G	**1119**w	NNB528H	**1148**w	NNB553H	**1175**	ONF863H	**1204**	SRJ327H
1093w	LNA193G	**1120**w	NNB529H	**1149**w	NNB554H	**1176**	ONF864H	**1205**w	SRJ328H
1094w	LNA194G	**1121**w	NNB530H	**1150**	NNB555H	**1177**	ONF865H	**1206**	SRJ329H
1095w	LNA195G	**1122**w	NNB531H	**1151**	NNB556H	**1178**	ONF866H	**1207**w	SRJ330H
1096w	LNA196G	**1123**	NNB532H	**1161**	ONF849H	**1179**	ONF867H	**1208**t	SRJ331H
1097w	LNA197G	**1124**	NNB533H	**1162**	ONF850H	**1180**	ONF868H	**1211**w	SRJ334H
1104w	NNB513H	**1125**w	NNB534H	**1163**	ONF851H	**1182**	ONF870H	**1212**w	SRJ335H
1105w	NNB514H	**1126**w	NNB535H	**1164**	ONF852H	**1183**	ONF871H	**1214**w	SRJ337H
1106w	NNB515H	**1132**w	NNB537H	**1165**	ONF853H	**1184**	ONF872H	**1215**w	SRJ338H
1107w	NNB516H	**1133**w	NNB538H	**1166**	ONF854H	**1185**	ONF873H	**1216**w	SRJ339H
1108	NNB517H	**1134**w	NNB539H	**1167**	ONF855H	**1186**	ONF874H	**1218**	SRJ341H
1110w	NNB519H	**1136**t	NNB541H	**1168**	ONF856H	**1187**	ONF875H	**1219**	SRJ342H
1111	NNB520H	**1138**w	NNB543H	**1169**	ONF857H	**1188**	ONF876H		

t Training bus

1300–1319

Chassis Leyland National 1051/1R/0502 (1319: 1051/1R)
Bodywork Leyland National B41F

Built 1974
Number in Stock 19

1300	XVU367M	**1304**	XVU371M	**1308**	XVU375M	**1312**	XVU379M	**1317**	XVU384M
1301	XVU368M	**1305**	XVU372M	**1309**	XVU376M	**1313**	XVU380M	**1318**	XVU385M
1302	XVU369M	**1306**	XVU373M	**1310**	XVU377M	**1315**	XVU382M	**1319**	GND511N
1303	XVU370M	**1307**	XVU374M	**1311**	XVU378M	**1316**	XVU383M		

1330–1341

Chassis Leyland National 1151/2R/0202
(1336/7: 1151/2R/2802, 1338–41: 1051/2R/2804)
Bodywork Leyland National B45D
(1330: B43D, 1338-41: B39D)

Built 1972/3
Number in Stock 12

No. 1330 is the first production Leyland National

1330	TXJ507K	**1333**	TXJ510K	**1336**	TXJ513K	**1338**	VVM601L	**1340**	VVM603L
1331	TXJ508K	**1334**	TXJ511K	**1337**	TXJ514K	**1339**	VVM602L	**1341**	VVM604L
1332	TXJ509K	**1335**	TXJ512K						

1342–1353

Chassis Metro Scania BR111MH (1350-3 BR110MH)
Bodywork Metro-Cammell Weymann B44D (1350-31 B40D)

Built 1972/3
Number in Stock 12

1342	TXJ515K	**1345**w	TXJ518K	**1348**	TXJ521K	**1350**w	VVM605L	**1352**	VVM607L
1343	TXJ516K	**1346**	TXJ519K	**1349**	TXJ522K	**1351**	VVM606L	**1353**w	VVM608L
1344w	TXJ517K	**1347**	TXJ520K						

1360

Chassis Metro Scania BR110MH
Bodywork Metro-Cammell Weymann B40D

Built 1973
Number in Stock 1

1360 VVM609L

1400–1424

Chassis Bristol VRT/SL2/6LX
Bodywork Eastern Coachworks H43/32F

Built 1973
Number in Stock 25

1400	AJA400L	**1405**	AJA405L	**1410**	AJA410L	**1415**	AJA415L	**1420**	AJA420L
1401	AJA401L	**1406**	AJA406L	**1411**	AJA411L	**1416**	AJA416L	**1421**	AJA421L
1402	AJA402L	**1407**	AJA407L	**1412**	AJA412L	**1417**	AJA417L	**1422**	AJA422L
1403	AJA403L	**1408**	AJA408L	**1413**	AJA413L	**1418**	AJA418L	**1423**	AJA423L
1404	AJA404L	**1409**	AJA409L	**1414**	AJA414L	**1419**	AJA419L	**1424**	AJA424L

1425–1434

Chassis Metropolitan BR111DH
Bodywork Metro-Cammell Weymann H44/29F

Built 1974
Number in Stock 10

1425w	GNC277N	**1427**w	GNC279N	**1429**w	GNC281N	**1431**w	GNC283N	**1433**w	GNC285N
1426w	GNC278N	**1428**w	GNC280N	**1430**w	GNC282N	**1432**w	GNC284N	**1434**w	GNC286N

1435/1436

Chassis Foden-NC
Bodywork Northern Counties H43/32F

Built 1976
Number in Stock 2

1435w LNA258P **1436**w PNE358R

1437–1440

Chassis Dennis Dominator DD110 (1439/40: DDA136)
Bodywork Northern Counties H43/32F

Built 1980/1
Number in Stock 4

1437 HDB437V **1438** HDB438V **1439** TND439X **1440** TND440X

1446–1448

Chassis Volvo Ailsa B55–10
Bodywork Northern Counties H44/35F

Built 1980/2
Number in Stock 3

1446 NNA134W **1447** WRJ447X **1448** WRJ448X

1451

Chassis Leyland (Bristol) Olympian B45 TL11/1R
Bodywork Northern Counties H43/30F

Built 1980
Number in Stock 1

1451 NJA568W

1461/1462

Chassis Scania BR112DH
Bodywork Northern Counties H/F

Built On order for 1983
Number in Stock nil

1461 FWH461Y **1462** FWH462Y

1685–1687

Chassis Leyland Panther PSUR1A/1R
Bodywork Northern Counties B45D
Acquired from Wigan Corporation (85/7) in 1974

Built 1970
Number in Stock 2

1685w HJP955H **1687**w HJP957H

1704–1742

Chassis Seddon IV
Bodywork Seddon B19F (1704-14: B23F)

Built 1973-5
Number in Stock 32

1704a	XVU334M	**1718**	XVU348M	**1725**a	XVU355M	**1731**	XVU361M	**1737**b	HJA121N
1708w	XVU338M	**1719**	XVU349M	**1726**	XVU356M	**1732**	XVU362M	**1738**	HJA122N
1711a	XVU341M	**1720**	XVU350M	**1727**	XVU357M	**1733**	XVU363M	**1739**	HJA123N
1714a	XVU344M	**1721**	XVU351M	**1728**	XVU358M	**1734**	XVU364M	**1740**	HJA124N
1715	XVU345M	**1722**	XVU352M	**1729**x	XVU359M	**1735**w	BNE729N	**1741**	HJA125N
1716	XVU346M	**1723**	XVU353M	**1730**	XVU360M	**1736**w	GND509N	**1742**	HJA126N
1717	XVU347M	**1724**	XVU354M						

a Revenue Protection Squad bus b Data Collectors Bus
x Experimental battery/diesel bus – not licensed for public service.

1743/1744

Chassis Ford Transit
Bodywork Reeves Burgess B17F

Built 1979
Number in Stock 2

1743w	CNF1T	**1744**w	CNF2T

1745–1748

Chassis Bedford CF
Bodywork Reeves Burgess B17F

Built 1978
Number in Stock 4

1745w	AJA3T	**1746**w	AJA4T	**1747**w	XRJ9S	**1748**a	WNE10S

a On loan to Crosville

2018

Chassis Daimler Fleetline CRG6LX
Bodywork Park Royal H45/28D
Acquired from Manchester Corporation (2018) in 1969

Built 1968
Number in Stock 1

2018w	HVM818F

2051–2304

Chassis Daimler Fleetline CRG6LXB-33
(2051-83: CRG6LX-33)
Bodywork Park Royal H47/28D (2051-2144)
Metro-Cammell Weymann H47/29D (2151-2209)
Park Royal H47/28D (2211-70)
Roe H47/28D (2271-2304)
2051-95 acquired from Manchester Corporation
(same numbers) in 1969

Built 1969-72
Number in Stock 185

2051w	LNA251G	**2142**w	NNB601H	**2190**	PNA229J	**2229**	RNA229J	**2268**	RNA268J
2071w	LNA271G	**2144**w	NNB603H	**2191**	PNA230J	**2231**	RNA231J	**2269**	RNA269J
2078w	LNA278G	**2151**	ONF883H	**2192**	PNA231J	**2232**	RNA232J	**2270**	RNA270J
2095w	LNA295G	**2152**	ONF884H	**2193**	PNA232J	**2234**	RNA234J	**2271**	SVR271K
2102t	NNB561H	**2154**	ONF886H	**2194**	PNA233J	**2235**	RNA235J	**2272**	SVR272K
2103t	NNB562H	**2155**	ONF887H	**2195**	PNA234J	**2236**	RNA236J	**2273**	SVR273K
2104w	NNB563H	**2156**	ONF888H	**2196**w	PNA235J	**2237**	RNA237J	**2274**	SVR274K
2105w	NNB564H	**2157**	ONF889H	**2197**	PNA236J	**2238**	RNA238J	**2275**	SVR275K
2106w	NNB565H	**2158**	ONF890H	**2198**	PNA237J	**2239**	RNA239J	**2276**	SVR276K
2108	NNB567H	**2160**	ONF892H	**2199**	PNA238J	**2240**	RNA240J	**2277**	SVR277K
2110w	NNB569H	**2162**	PNA201J	**2200**	PNA239J	**2241**	RNA241J	**2278**	SVR278K
2111w	NNB570H	**2163**	PNA202J	**2201**	PNA240J	**2242**	RNA242J	**2279**	SVR279K
2112	NNB571H	**2164**	PNA203J	**2202**	PNA241J	**2243**	RNA243J	**2280**	SVR280K
2114	NNB573H	**2165**	PNA204J	**2203**	PNA242J	**2244**	RNA244J	**2281**	SVR281K
2115w	NNB574H	**2166**	PNA205J	**2204**	PNA243J	**2245**	RNA245J	**2282**	SVR282K
2116w	NNB575H	**2167**	PNA206J	**2205**	PNA244J	**2246**	RNA246J	**2283**	SVR283K
2117w	NNB576H	**2168**	PNA207J	**2206**	PNA245J	**2247**	RNA247J	**2284**	SVR284K
2119w	NNB578H	**2169**	PNA208J	**2207**	PNA246J	**2248**	RNA248J	**2285**	SVR285K
2121	NNB580H	**2170**	PNA209J	**2208**	PNA247J	**2249**	RNA249J	**2286**	SVR286K
2122	NNB581H	**2171**	PNA210J	**2209**	PNA248J	**2250**	RNA250J	**2287**	SVR287K
2123	NNB582H	**2172**	PNA211J	**2211**	RNA211J	**2251**	RNA251J	**2288**	SVR288K
2124w	NNB583H	**2173**	PNA212J	**2212**	RNA212J	**2252**	RNA252J	**2289**	SVR289K
2125	NNB584H	**2174**	PNA213J	**2213**	RNA213J	**2253**	RNA253J	**2290**	SVR290K
2126w	NNB585H	**2175**	PNA214J	**2214**	RNA214J	**2254**	RNA254J	**2291**	SVR291K
2128	NNB587H	**2177**	PNA216J	**2215**	RNA215J	**2255**	RNA255J	**2292**	SVR292K
2129	NNB588H	**2178**	PNA217J	**2216**	RNA216J	**2256**	RNA256J	**2293**	SVR293K
2130w	NNB589H	**2179**	PNA218J	**2217**	RNA217J	**2257**	RNA257J	**2294**	SVR294K
2131	NNB590H	**2180**	PNA219J	**2218**	RNA218J	**2258**	RNA258J	**2295**	SVR295K
2132w	NNB591H	**2181**	PNA220J	**2219**	RNA219J	**2259**	RNA259J	**2296**	SVR296K
2133w	NNB592H	**2182**	PNA221J	**2220**	RNA220J	**2260**	RNA260J	**2297**	SVR297K
2134w	NNB593H	**2183**	PNA222J	**2221**	RNA221J	**2261**	RNA261J	**2298**	SVR298K
2135w	NNB594H	**2184**	PNA223J	**2222**	RNA222J	**2262**	RNA262J	**2299**	SVR299K
2136w	NNB595H	**2185**	PNA224J	**2223**	RNA223J	**2263**	RNA263J	**2300**	SVR300K
2137w	NNB596H	**2186**	PNA225J	**2224**	RNA224J	**2264**	RNA264J	**2301**	SVR301K
2138	NNB597H	**2187**	PNA226J	**2226**	RNA226J	**2265**	RNA265J	**2302**	SVR302K
2139	NNB598H	**2188**	PNA227J	**2227**	RNA227J	**2266**	RNA266J	**2303**	SVR303K
2140	NNB599H	**2189**	PNA228J	**2228**	RNA228J	**2267**	RNA267J	**2304**	SVR304K

t Training bus

2318–2337

Chassis Daimler Fleetline CRL6 (2332-7: CRG6LXB)
Bodywork Park Royal H44/27F (2318-26/8/9/31)
Metro-Cammell Weymann H44/27F(2327/30/2-7)
Acquired from Lancashire United (318-37) in 1981
Originally London Transport Executive DMS597/84/8/91, 603/15/22/34/5, 1407, 632/75, 1489, 710, 1452/8/60/2/5/6

Built 1973
Number in Stock 20

2318	MLK597L	**2322**	MLK603L	**2326**	MLK635L	**2330**	MLH489L	**2334**	MLH460L
2319	MLK584L	**2323**	MLK615L	**2327**	MLH407L	**2331**	TGX710M	**2335**	MLH462L
2320	MLK588L	**2324**	MLK622L	**2328**	MLK632L	**2332**	MLH452L	**2336**	MLH465L
2321	MLK591L	**2325**	MLK634L	**2329**	MLK675L	**2333**	MLH458L	**2337**	MLH466L

2358–2413

Chassis Daimler Fleetline CRG6LXB-33
Bodywork Northern Counties H49/27D
(2394/8-400/3: H47/32F, 2395-7/401/2: H47/29D)
Acquired from Lancashire United (358-63/94-413) in 1981

Built 1970-4
Number in Stock 26

2358	ATJ272J	**2394**	RTJ422L	**2399**	RTJ427L	**2404**	VTC494M	**2409**	VTC499M
2359	ATJ273J	**2395**	RTJ423L	**2400**	RTJ428L	**2405**	VTC495M	**2410**	VTC500M
2360w	ATJ274J	**2396**	RTJ424L	**2401**	RTJ429L	**2406**	VTC496M	**2411**	VTC501M
2361w	ATJ275J	**2397**	RTJ425L	**2402**	RTJ430L	**2407**	VTC497M	**2412**	VTC502M
2362w	ATJ276J	**2398**	RTJ426L	**2403**	RTJ431L	**2408**	VTC498M	**2413**	VTC503M
2363w	ATJ277J								

3001

Chassis Leyland (Bristol) Olympian ONTL11/1R
Bodywork Northern Counties H43/30F
This batch will continue to 3025, some being to type ONLXB/1R

Built 1982
Number in Stock 1

3001	ANA1Y	**3006**	ANA6Y	**3011**	ANA11Y	**3016**	ANA16Y	**3021**	ANA21Y
3002	ANA2Y	**3007**	ANA7Y	**3012**	ANA12Y	**3017**	ANA17Y	**3022**	ANA22Y
3003	ANA3Y	**3008**	ANA8Y	**3013**	ANA13Y	**3018**	ANA18Y	**3023**	ANA23Y
3004	ANA4Y	**3009**	ANA9Y	**3014**	ANA14Y	**3019**	ANA19Y	**3024**	ANA24Y
3005	ANA5Y	**3010**	ANA10Y	**3015**	ANA15Y	**3020**	ANA20Y	**3025**	ANA25Y

3050

Chassis Leyland Titan PD2/40
Bodywork Metro-Cammell H36/28F
Acquired from Salford Corporation (201) in 1969

Built 1964
Number in Stock 1

3050t ARJ201B

t Training bus

3270–3281

Chassis Leyland Titan PD2A/27 (3281: PD2/37)
Bodywork Massey H37/27F
Acquired from Wigan Corporation (146/0) in 1974

Built 1964/6
Number in Stock 2

3270t AEK1B **3281**t DEK3D

t Training bus

3310–3339

Chassis Leyland Atlantean PDR2/1 (3330-9: AN68/2R)
Bodywork Northern Counties H48/31D
Acquired from Wigan Corporation (92-7, 151-6, 1-10) in 1974

Built 1971/2
Number in Stock 22

3310w	KJP20J	**3315**	KJP25J	**3320**	KJP30J	**3332**	NEK3K	**3336**	NEK7K
3311w	KJP21J	**3316**w	KJP26J	**3321**	KJP31J	**3333**	NEK4K	**3337**	NEK8K
3312	KJP22J	**3317**w	KJP27J	**3330**	NEK1K	**3334**	NEK5K	**3338**	NEK9K
3313w	KJP23J	**3318**	KJP28J	**3331**	NEK2K	**3335**	NEK6K	**3339**	NEK10K
3314	KJP24J	**3319**	KJP29J						

3820

Chassis Leyland Atlantean PDR1/2
Bodywork Metro-Cammell H43/32F
Acquired from Manchester Corporation (3820) in 1969

Built 1966
Number in Stock 1

3820t	END820D

t Training bus

4001–4015

Chassis Leyland Titan TNLXB1RF (4003/12-5: TNTL111RF)
Bodywork Park Royal H47/26F

Built 1978-80
Number in Stock 15

4001	ANE1T	**4004**	ANE4T	**4007**	GNF7V	**4010**	GNF10V	**4013**	GNF13V
4002	ANE2T	**4005**	ANE5T	**4008**	GNF8V	**4011**	GNF11V	**4014**	GNF14V
4003	FVR3V	**4006**	GNF6V	**4009**	GNF9V	**4012**	GNF12V	**4015**	GNF15V

4661–4750

Chassis Daimler Fleetline CRG6LX
Bodywork Metro-Cammell H43/33F (4661/2)
Metro-Cammell Weymann H43/33F (4745/50)
Acquired from Manchester Corporation (same numbers) in 1969

Built 1964-7
Number in Stock 4

4661t	ANA661B	**4662**t	ANA662B	**4745**t	FNE745D	**4750**t	FNE750D

t Training bus

5001–5170

Chassis Metro-Cammell Weymann Metrobus DR101/6 (5001-10)
DR102/10 (5011-30), DR102/21 (5031-110),
DR102/23 (5111-70)
Bodywork Metro-Cammell Weymann H43/30F
Batch will continue to 5190

Built 1979-82
Number in Stock 170

5001	GBU1V	**5035**	MRJ35W	**5069**	MRJ69W	**5103**	SND103X	**5137**	SND137X
5002	GBU2V	**5036**	MRJ36W	**5070**	MRJ70W	**5104**	SND104X	**5138**	SND138X
5003	GBU3V	**5037**	MRJ37W	**5071**	ORJ71W	**5105**	SND105X	**5139**	SND139X
5004	GBU4V	**5038**	MRJ38W	**5072**	ORJ72W	**5106**	SND106X	**5140**	SND140X
5005	GBU5V	**5039**	MRJ39W	**5073**	ORJ73W	**5107**	SND107X	**5141**	SND141X
5006	GBU6V	**5040**	MRJ40W	**5074**	ORJ74W	**5108**	SND108X	**5142**	SND142X
5007	GBU7V	**5041**	MRJ41W	**5075**	ORJ75W	**5109**	SND109X	**5143**	SND143X
5008	GBU8V	**5042**	MRJ42W	**5076**	ORJ76W	**5110**	SND110X	**5144**	SND144X
5009	GBU9V	**5043**	MRJ43W	**5077**	ORJ77W	**5111**	SND111X	**5145**	SND145X
5010	GBU10V	**5044**	MRJ44W	**5078**	ORJ78W	**5112**	SND112X	**5146**	SND146X
5011	GBU11V	**5045**	MRJ45W	**5079**	ORJ79W	**5113**	SND113X	**5147**	SND147X
5012	GBU12V	**5046**	MRJ46W	**5080**	ORJ80W	**5114**	SND114X	**5148**	SND148X
5013	GBU13V	**5047**	MRJ47W	**5081**	ORJ81W	**5115**	SND115X	**5149**	SND149X
5014	GBU14V	**5048**	MRJ48W	**5082**	ORJ82W	**5116**	SND116X	**5150**	SND150X
5015	GBU15V	**5049**	MRJ49W	**5083**	ORJ83W	**5117**	SND117X	**5151**	ANA151Y
5016	GBU16V	**5050**	MRJ50W	**5084**	ORJ84W	**5118**	SND118X	**5152**	ANA152Y
5017	GBU17V	**5051**	MRJ51W	**5085**	ORJ85W	**5119**	SND119X	**5153**	ANA153Y
5018	MNC494W	**5052**	MRJ52W	**5086**	ORJ86W	**5120**	SND120X	**5154**	ANA154Y
5019	MNC495W	**5053**	MRJ53W	**5087**	ORJ87W	**5121**	SND121X	**5155**	ANA155Y
5020	GBU20V	**5054**	MRJ54W	**5088**	ORJ88W	**5122**	SND122X	**5156**	ANA156Y
5021	MNC496W	**5055**	MRJ55W	**5089**	ORJ89W	**5123**	SND123X	**5157**	ANA157Y
5022	GBU22V	**5056**	MRJ56W	**5090**	ORJ90W	**5124**	SND124X	**5158**	ANA158Y
5023	MNC497W	**5057**	MRJ57W	**5091**	ORJ91W	**5125**	SND125X	**5159**	ANA159Y
5024	GBU24V	**5058**	MRJ58W	**5092**	ORJ92W	**5126**	SND126X	**5160**	ANA160Y
5025	GBU25V	**5059**	MRJ59W	**5093**	ORJ93W	**5127**	SND127X	**5161**	ANA161Y
5026	MNC498W	**5060**	MRJ60W	**5094**	ORJ94W	**5128**	SND128X	**5162**	ANA162Y
5027	GBU27V	**5061**	MRJ61W	**5095**	ORJ95W	**5129**	SND129X	**5163**	ANA163Y
5028	GBU28V	**5062**	MRJ62W	**5096**	ORJ96W	**5130**	SND130X	**5164**	ANA164Y
5029	GBU29V	**5063**	MRJ63W	**5097**	ORJ97W	**5131**	SND131X	**5165**	ANA165Y
5030	MNC499W	**5064**	MRJ64W	**5098**	ORJ98W	**5132**	SND132X	**5166**	ANA166Y
5031	MRJ31W	**5065**	MRJ65W	**5099**	ORJ99W	**5133**	SND133X	**5167**	ANA167Y
5032	MRJ32W	**5066**	MRJ66W	**5100**	ORJ100W	**5134**	SND134X	**5168**	ANA168Y
5033	MRJ33W	**5067**	MRJ67W	**5101**	SND101X	**5135**	SND135X	**5169**	ANA169Y
5034	MRJ34W	**5068**	MRJ68W	**5102**	SND102X	**5136**	SND136X	**5170**	ANA170Y

5191–5199

Chassis Leyland Atlantean PDR1A/1
Bodywork Roe H43/31D

Built 1970/1
Number in Stock 7

5191 ABU191J
5192 ABU192J
5193 ABU193J
5194 ABU194J
5196 ABU196J
5197 ABU197J
5199w ABU199J

5466–5471

Chassis Leyland Atlantean PDR1A/1
Bodywork Northern Counties H43/32F

Built 1970/1
Number in Stock 6

5466 PNF941J
5467 PNF942J
5468 PNF943J
5469 PNF944J
5470 PNF945J
5471 PNF946J

5628

Chassis Daimler Fleetline CRG6LX
Bodywork Northern Counties H42/32F
Acquired from SHMD Joint Board (28) in 1969

Built 1966
Number in Stock 1

5628t NMA328D

t Training bus

5811–5852

Chassis Leyland Titan PD2/40
Bodywork East Lancs H36/28R
Acquired from Stockport Corporation (11, 21/5/8, 31-3, 50) in 1969

Built 1964-7
Number in Stock 9

5811w BJA911B
5821w BJA921B
5825w BJA925B
5828t FDB328C
5831w FDB331C
5832t FDB332C
5833w FDB333C
5850t HJA950E
5852t HJA952E

t Training bus

5886–5896

Chassis Leyland Titan PD3/14
Bodywork East Lancs H38/32R
(5893-6: H38/32F)
Acquired from Stockport Corporation (86, 93/4/6) in 1969

Built 1969
Number in Stock 4

5886t MJA886G
5893w MJA893G
5894t MJA894G
5896t MJA896G

t Training bus

6245–6254

Chassis Daimler Fleetline CRG6LXB
Bodywork Northern Countries H43/32F
(6250-4: H45/27D)

Built 1972
Number in Stock 10

6245 TNB747K
6246 TNB748K
6247 TNB749K
6248 TNB750K
6249 TNB751K
6250 TNB757K
6251 TNB758K
6252 TNB759K
6253 TNB760K
6254 TNB761K

6346–6350

Chassis Daimler Fleetline CRG6LX
Bodywork East Lancs H45/26D

Built 1970/1
Number in Stock 4

6346w NEN506J
6347w NEN507J
6349 NEN509J
6350 NEN510J

6395–6399

Chassis Daimler Fleetline CRG6LXB
Bodywork Northern Counties H43/32F

Built 1972
Number in Stock 5

6395 TNB752K
6396 TNB753K
6397 TNB754K
6398 TNB755K
6399 TNB756K

6654

Chassis Leyland Titan PD3/4
Bodywork East Lancs H41/32F
Acquired from Bolton Corporation (154) in 1969

Built 1961
Number in Stock 1

6654w SBN754

6774–6816

Chassis Leyland Atlantean PDR1A/1 (6802-16: PDR2/1)
Bodywork East Lancs H45/33F (6774/7),
H43/27D (6791-801), H49/37F (6802-16)
6774/7/91/800 Acquired from Bolton Corporation
(274/7/91, 300) in 1969

Built 1968-72
Number in Stock 21

6774w	MWH274G	**6801**w	OBN301H	**6805**	TWH805K	**6809**	TWH809K	**6813**	TWH813K
6777w	MWH277G	**6802**	TWH802K	**6806**	TWH806K	**6810**	TWH810K	**6814**	TWH814K
6791w	OBN291H	**6803**	TWH803K	**6807**	TWH807K	**6811**	TWH811K	**6815**	TWH815K
6798w	OBN298H	**6804**	TWH804K	**6808**	TWH808K	**6812**	TWH812K	**6816**	TWH816K
6800w	OBN300H								

6901–6990

Chassis Leyland Fleetline FE30GR (6901-10),
FE30AGR (6911-90)
Bodywork Northern Counties H43/32F Mark 1a Standard
Acquired from Lancashire United (485-529/42/70-613) in 1981

Built 1977-80
Number in Stock 90

6901	OBN502R	**6919**	PTD647S	**6937**	TWH696T	**6955**	YTE592V	**6973**	DWH689W
6902	OBN503R	**6920**	PTD648S	**6938**	TWH697T	**6956**	YTE593V	**6974**	DWH690W
6903	OBN504R	**6921**	PTD649S	**6939**	TWH698T	**6957**	BCB610V	**6975**	DWH691W
6904	OBN505R	**6922**	PTD650S	**6940**	TWH699T	**6958**	BCB611V	**6976**	DWH692W
6905	OBN506R	**6923**	PTD651S	**6941**	TWH700T	**6959**	BCB612V	**6977**	DWH693W
6906	OBN507R	**6924**	PTD652S	**6942**	TWH701T	**6960**	BCB613V	**6978**	DWH694W
6907	OBN508R	**6925**	PTD653S	**6943**	TWH702T	**6961**	BCB614V	**6979**	DWH695W
6908	OBN509R	**6926**	PTD654S	**6944**	TWH703T	**6962**	BCB615V	**6980**	DWH696W
6909	OBN510R	**6927**	PTD655S	**6945**	TWH704T	**6963**	BCB616V	**6981**	DWH697W
6910	OBN511R	**6928**	PTD656S	**6946**	WWH94T	**6964**	BCB617V	**6982**	DWH698W
6911	PTD639S	**6929**	PTD657S	**6947**	YTE584V	**6965**	BCB618V	**6983**	DWH699W
6912a	PTD640S	**6930**	PTD658S	**6948**	YTE585V	**6966**	DWH682W	**6984**	DWH700W
6913	PTD641S	**6931**	TWH690T	**6949**	YTE586V	**6967**	DWH683W	**6985**	DWH701W
6914	PTD642S	**6932**	TWH691T	**6950**	YTE587V	**6968**	DWH684W	**6986**	DWH702W
6915	PTD643S	**6933**	TWH692T	**6951**	YTE588V	**6969**	DWH685W	**6987**	DWH703W
6916	PTD644S	**6934**	TWH693T	**6952**	YTE589V	**6970**	DWH686W	**6988**	DWH704W
6917	PTD645S	**6935**	TWH694T	**6953**	YTE590V	**6971**	DWH687W	**6989**	DWH705W
6918	PTD646S	**6936**	TWH695T	**6954**	YTE591V	**6972**	DWH688W	**6990**	DWH706W

a Rebodied Northern Counties H43/32F light alloy Standard, 1983

7001–7150

Chassis Leyland Atlantean AN68/1R
Bodywork Park Royal H43/32F (7001-145) (7032: 043/32F)
Northern Counties H43/32F (7146-50)
Mark I Standard

Built 1972/3
Number in Stock 150

7001	VNB101L	**7031**	VNB131L	**7061**	VNB161L	**7091**	WBN969L	**7121**	XJA512L
7002	VNB102L	**7032**	VNB132L	**7062**	VNB162L	**7092**	WBN970L	**7122**	XJA513L
7003	VNB103L	**7033**	VNB133L	**7063**	VNB163L	**7093**	WBN971L	**7123**	XJA514L
7004	VNB104L	**7034**	VNB134L	**7064**	VNB164L	**7094**	WBN972L	**7124**	XJA515L
7005	VNB105L	**7035**	VNB135L	**7065**	VNB165L	**7095**	WBN973L	**7125**	XJA516L
7006	VNB106L	**7036**	VNB136L	**7066**	VNB166L	**7096**	WBN974L	**7126**	XJA517L
7007	VNB107L	**7037**	VNB137L	**7067**	VNB167L	**7097**	WBN975L	**7127**	XJA518L
7008	VNB108L	**7038**	VNB138L	**7068**	VNB168L	**7098**	WBN976L	**7128**	XJA519L
7009	VNB109L	**7039**	VNB139L	**7069**	VNB169L	**7099**	WBN977L	**7129**	XJA520L
7010	VNB110L	**7040**	VNB140L	**7070**	VNB170L	**7100**	WBN978L	**7130**	XJA521L
7011	VNB111L	**7041**	VNB141L	**7071**	VNB171L	**7101**	WBN979L	**7131**	XJA522L
7012	VNB112L	**7042**	VNB142L	**7072**	WBN950L	**7102**	WBN980L	**7132**	XJA523L
7013	VNB113L	**7043**	VNB143L	**7073**	WBN951L	**7103**	WBN981L	**7133**	XJA524L
7014	VNB114L	**7044**	VNB144L	**7074**	WBN952L	**7104**	WBN982L	**7134**	XJA525L
7015	VNB115L	**7045**	VNB145L	**7075**	WBN953L	**7105**	WBN983L	**7135**	XJA526L
7016	VNB116L	**7046**	VNB146L	**7076**	WBN954L	**7106**	WBN984L	**7136**	XJA527L
7017	VNB117L	**7047**	VNB147L	**7077**	WBN955L	**7107**	WBN985L	**7137**	XJA528L
7018	VNB118L	**7048**	VNB148L	**7078**	WBN956L	**7108**	WBN986L	**7138**	XJA529L
7019	VNB119L	**7049**	VNB149L	**7079**	WBN957L	**7109**	WBN987L	**7139**	XJA530L
7020	VNB120L	**7050**	VNB150L	**7080**	WBN958L	**7110**	XJA501L	**7140**	XJA531L
7021	VNB121L	**7051**	VNB151L	**7081**	WBN959L	**7111**	XJA502L	**7141**	XJA532L
7022	VNB122L	**7052**	VNB152L	**7082**	WBN960L	**7112**	XJA503L	**7142**	XJA533L
7023	VNB123L	**7053**	VNB153L	**7083**	WBN961L	**7113**	XJA504L	**7143**	XJA534L
7024	VNB124L	**7054**	VNB154L	**7084**	WBN962L	**7114**	XJA505L	**7144**	XJA535L
7025	VNB125L	**7055**	VNB155L	**7085**	WBN963L	**7115**	XJA506L	**7145**	XJA536L
7026	VNB126L	**7056**	VNB156L	**7086**	WBN964L	**7116**	XJA507L	**7146**	VNB172L
7027	VNB127L	**7057**	VNB157L	**7087**	WBN965L	**7117**	XJA508L	**7147**	VNB173L
7028	VNB128L	**7058**	VNB158L	**7088**	WBN966L	**7118**	XJA509L	**7148**	VNB174L
7029	VNB129L	**7059**	VNB159L	**7089**	WBN967L	**7119**	XJA510L	**7149**	VNB175L
7030	VNB130L	**7060**	VNB160L	**7090**	WBN968L	**7120**	XJA511L	**7150**	VNB176L

7151–7205

Chassis Daimler Fleetline CRG6LXB
Bodywork Park Royal H43/32F Mark I Standard

Built 1973
Number in Stock 55

7151	WBN988L	7162	WBN999L	7173	WWH31L	7184	WWH42L	7195	XJA545L
7152	WBN989L	7163	WWH21L	7174	WWH32L	7185	WWH43L	7196	XJA546L
7153	WBN990L	7164	WWH22L	7175	WWH33L	7186	WWH44L	7197	XJA547L
7154	WBN991L	7165	WWH23L	7176	WWH34L	7187	XJA537L	7198	XJA548L
7155	WBN992L	7166	WWH24L	7177	WWH35L	7188	XJA538L	7199	XJA549L
7156	WBN993L	7167	WWH25L	7178	WWH36L	7189	XJA539L	7200	XJA550L
7157	WBN994L	7168	WWH26L	7179	WWH37L	7190	XJA540L	7201	XJA551L
7158	WBN995L	7169	WWH27L	7180	WWH38L	7191	XJA541L	7202	XJA552L
7159	WBN996L	7170	WWH28L	7181	WWH39L	7192	XJA542L	7203	XJA553L
7160	WBN997L	7171	WWH29L	7182	WWH40L	7193	XJA543L	7204	XJA554L
7161	WBN998L	7172	WWH30L	7183	WWH41L	7194	XJA544L	7205	XJA555L

7206–7500

Chassis Daimler Fleetline CRG6LXB
(7383/91-6/8-500 were built at Leyland)
Bodywork Northern Counties H45/27D (7206-51/80/1)
Northern Counties H43/32F (7252-79/82-500)
7206-347/9-99 Mark 1 Standard
7348/400-500 Mark 1a Standard

Built 1972-6
Number in Stock 295

7206	VNB177L	7265	VNB236L	7324	XJA580L	7383	YNA338M	7442	GND508N
7207	VNB178L	7266	VNB237L	7325	YNA280M	7384	YNA339M	7443	GDB162N
7208	VNB179L	7267	VNB238L	7326	YNA281M	7385	YNA340M	7444	GDB163N
7209	VNB180L	7268	VNB239L	7327	YNA282M	7386	YNA341M	7445	GDB164N
7210	VNB181L	7269	VNB240L	7328	YNA283M	7387	YNA342M	7446	GDB165N
7211	VNB182L	7270	VNB241L	7329	YNA284M	7388	YNA343M	7447	GDB166N
7212	VNB183L	7271	YNA271M	7330	YNA285M	7389	YNA344M	7448	HJA116N
7213	VNB184L	7272	YNA272M	7331	YNA286M	7390	YNA345M	7449	HJA117N
7214	VNB185L	7273	YNA273M	7332	YNA287M	7391	YNA346M	7450	HJA118N
7215	VNB186L	7274	YNA274M	7333	YNA288M	7392	YNA347M	7451	HJA119N
7216	VNB187L	7275	YNA275M	7334	YNA289M	7393	YNA348M	7452	HJA120N
7217	VNB188L	7276	YNA276M	7335	YNA290M	7394	YNA349M	7453	JND981N
7218	VNB189L	7277	YNA277M	7336	YNA291M	7395	YNA350M	7454	JND982N
7219	VNB190L	7278	YNA278M	7337	YNA292M	7396	YNA351M	7455	JND983N
7220	VNB191L	7279	YNA279M	7338	YNA293M	7397	YNA352M	7456	JDB108N
7221	VNB192L	7280	WWH45L	7339	YNA294M	7398	YNA353M	7457	JDB109N
7222	VNB193L	7281	WWH46L	7340	YNA295M	7399	YNA354M	7458	JDB110N
7223	VNB194L	7282	WWH47L	7341	YNA296M	7400	YNA355M	7459	JDB111N
7224	VNB195L	7283	WWH48L	7342	YNA297M	7401	YNA356M	7460	JVM991N
7225	VNB196L	7284	WWH49L	7343	YNA298M	7402	YNA357M	7461	JVM992N
7226	VNB197L	7285	WWH50L	7344	YNA299M	7403	YNA358M	7462	JVM993N
7227	VNB198L	7286	WWH51L	7345	YNA300M	7404	YNA359M	7463	JVM994N
7228	VNB199L	7287	WWH52L	7346	YNA301M	7405	YNA360M	7464	JVM995N
7229	VNB200L	7288	WWH53L	7347	YNA302M	7406	YNA361M	7465	KBU906P
7230	VNB201L	7289	WWH54L	7348	YNA303M	7407	YNA362M	7466	KBU907P
7231	VNB202L	7290	WWH55L	7349	YNA304M	7408	YNA363M	7467	KBU908P
7232	VNB203L	7291	WWH56L	7350	YNA305M	7409	YNA364M	7468	KBU909P
7233	VNB204L	7292a	WWH57L	7351	YNA306M	7410	YNA365M	7469	KBU910P
7234	VNB205L	7293	WWH58L	7352	YNA307M	7411	YNA366M	7470	LJA470P
7235	VNB206L	7294	WWH59L	7353	YNA308M	7412	YNA367M	7471	LJA471P
7236	VNB207L	7295	WWH60L	7354	YNA309M	7413	YNA368M	7472	LJA472P
7237	VNB208L	7296	WWH61L	7355	YNA310M	7414	YNA369M	7473	LJA473P
7238	VNB209L	7297	WWH62L	7356	YNA311M	7415	YNA370M	7474	LJA474P
7239	VNB210L	7298	WWH63L	7357	YNA312M	7416	BNE732N	7475	LJA475P
7240	VNB211L	7299	WWH64L	7358	YNA313M	7417	BNE733N	7476	LJA476P
7241	VNB212L	7300	XJA556L	7359	YNA314M	7418	BNE734N	7477	LJA477P
7242	VNB213L	7301	XJA557L	7360	YNA315M	7419	BNE735N	7478	LJA478P
7243	VNB214L	7302	XJA558L	7361	YNA316M	7420	BNE736N	7479	LJA479P
7244	VNB215L	7303	XJA559L	7362	YNA317M	7421	BNE737N	7480	LJA480P
7245	VNB216L	7304	XJA560L	7363	YNA318M	7422	GNC287N	7481	LJA481P
7246	VNB217L	7305	XJA561L	7364	YNA319M	7423	GNC288N	7482	LJA482P
7247	VNB218L	7306	XJA562L	7365	YNA320M	7424	BNE740N	7483	LJA483P
7248	VNB219L	7307	XJA563L	7366	YNA321M	7425	BNE741N	7484	LJA484P
7249	VNB220L	7308	XJA564L	7367	YNA322M	7426	BNE742N	7485	PRJ485R
7250	VNB221L	7309	XJA565L	7368	YNA323M	7427	GNC289N	7486	PRJ486R
7251	VNB222L	7310	XJA566L	7369	YNA324M	7428	GNC294N	7487	PRJ487R
7252	VNB223L	7311	XJA567L	7370	YNA325M	7429	GND489N	7488	PRJ488R
7253	VNB224L	7312	XJA568L	7371	YNA326M	7430	GND490N	7489	PRJ489R
7254	VNB225L	7313	XJA569L	7372	YNA327M	7431	GND491N	7490	PRJ490R
7255	VNB226L	7314	XJA570L	7373	YNA328M	7432	GND492N	7491	PRJ491R
7256	VNB227L	7315	XJA571L	7374	YNA329M	7433	GND493N	7492	PRJ492R
7257	VNB228L	7316	XJA572L	7375	YNA330M	7434	GND500N	7493	PRJ493R
7258	VNB229L	7317	XJA573L	7376	YNA331M	7435	GND501N	7494	PRJ494R
7259	VNB230L	7318	XJA574L	7377	YNA332M	7436	GND502N	7495	PRJ495R
7260	VNB231L	7319	XJA575L	7378	YNA333M	7437	GND503N	7496	PRJ496R
7261	VNB232L	7320	XJA576L	7379	YNA334M	7438	GND504N	7497	PRJ497R
7262	VNB233L	7321	XJA577L	7380	YNA335M	7439	GND505N	7498	PRJ498R
7263	VNB234L	7322	XJA578L	7381	YNA336M	7440	GND506N	7499	PRJ499R
7264	VNB235L	7323	XJA579L	7382	YNA337M	7441	GND507N	7500	PRJ500R

a Fitted with Sevcon gearbox.

7501–7800

Chassis Leyland Atlantean AN68/1R (7501-59), AN68A/1R (7560-800)
Bodywork Northern Counties H43/32F Mark Ia Standard
Built 1974-8
Number in Stock 300

7501	BNE751N	**7561**	JND985N	**7621**	LJA621P	**7681**	ONF681R	**7741**	SRJ741R
7502	BNE752N	**7562**	JND986N	**7622**	LJA622P	**7682**	ONF682R	**7742**	SRJ742R
7503	BNE753N	**7563**	JND987N	**7623**	LJA623P	**7683**	ONF683R	**7743**	SRJ743R
7504	BNE754N	**7564**	JND988N	**7624**	LJA624P	**7684**	ONF684R	**7744**	SRJ744R
7505	BNE755N	**7565**	JND989N	**7625**	LJA625P	**7685**	ONF685R	**7745**	SRJ745R
7506	BNE756N	**7566**	JND990N	**7626**	LJA626P	**7686**	ONF686R	**7746**	SRJ746R
7507	BNE757N	**7567**	JDB112N	**7627**	LJA627P	**7687**	ONF687R	**7747**	SRJ747R
7508	BNE758N	**7568**	JDB113N	**7628**	LJA628P	**7688**	ONF688R	**7748**	SRJ748R
7509	GNC290N	**7569**	JDB114N	**7629**	LJA629P	**7689**	ONF689R	**7749**	SRJ749R
7510	GNC291N	**7570**	JDB115N	**7630**	LJA630P	**7690**	ONF690R	**7750**	SRJ750R
7511	GNC292N	**7571**	KBU918P	**7631**	LJA631P	**7691**	ONF691R	**7751**	SRJ751R
7512	GNC293N	**7572**	JDB117N	**7632**	LJA632P	**7692**	ONF692R	**7752**	SRJ752R
7513	GND494N	**7573**	JDB118N	**7633**	LJA633P	**7693**	ONF693R	**7753**	SRJ753R
7514	GND495N	**7574**	JDB119N	**7634**	LJA634P	**7694**	ONF694R	**7754**	SRJ754R
7515	GND496N	**7575**	JDB120N	**7635**	LJA635P	**7695**	ONF695R	**7755**	SRJ755R
7516	GND497N	**7576**	JDB121N	**7636**	LJA636P	**7696**	ONF696R	**7756**	SRJ756R
7517	GND498N	**7577**	JDB122N	**7637**	LJA637P	**7697**	ONF697R	**7757**	SRJ757R
7518	GND499N	**7578**	JVM989N	**7638**	LJA638P	**7698**	ONF698R	**7758**	SRJ758R
7519	GND510N	**7579**	JVM990N	**7639**	LJA639P	**7699**	ONF699R	**7759**	SRJ759R
7520	GDB167N	**7580**	KBU911P	**7640**	LJA640P	**7700**	ONF700R	**7760**	SRJ760R
7521	GDB168N	**7581**	KBU912P	**7641**	LJA641P	**7701**	RJA701R	**7761**	UNA761S
7522	GDB169N	**7582**	KBU913P	**7642**	LJA642P	**7702**	RJA702R	**7762**	UNA762S
7523	GDB170N	**7583**	KBU914P	**7643**	LJA643P	**7703**	RJA703R	**7763**	UNA763S
7524	GDB171N	**7584**	KBU915P	**7644**	LJA644P	**7704**	RJA704R	**7764**	UNA764S
7525	GDB172N	**7585**	KBU916P	**7645**	LJA645P	**7705**	RJA705R	**7765**	UNA765S
7526	GDB173N	**7586**	KBU917P	**7646**	LJA646P	**7706**	RJA706R	**7766**	UNA766S
7527	GDB174N	**7587**	KDB680P	**7647**	LJA647P	**7707**	RJA707R	**7767**	UNA767S
7528	GDB175N	**7588**	KDB681P	**7648**	LJA648P	**7708**	RJA708R	**7768**	UNA768S
7529	GDB176N	**7589**	KDB682P	**7649**	LJA649P	**7709**	RJA709R	**7769**	UNA769S
7530	GDB177N	**7590**	KDB683P	**7650**	LJA650P	**7710**	RJA710R	**7770**	UNA770S
7531	GDB178N	**7591**	KDB684P	**7651**	LJA651P	**7711**	RJA711R	**7771**	UNA771S
7532	GDB179N	**7592**	KDB685P	**7652**	LJA652P	**7712**	RJA712R	**7772**	UNA772S
7533	GDB180N	**7593**	KDB686P	**7653**	ONF653R	**7713**	RJA713R	**7773**	UNA773S
7534	GDB181N	**7594**	KDB687P	**7654**	ONF654R	**7714**	RJA714R	**7774**	UNA774S
7535	HNB25N	**7595**	KDB688P	**7655**	ONF655R	**7715**	RJA715R	**7775**	UNA775S
7536	HNB26N	**7596**	KDB689P	**7656**	ONF656R	**7716**	RJA716R	**7776**	UNA776S
7537	HNB27N	**7597**	LNA250P	**7657**	ONF657R	**7717**	RJA717R	**7777**	UNA777S
7538	HNB28N	**7598**	LNA251P	**7658**	ONF658R	**7718**	RJA718R	**7778**	UNA778S
7539	HNB29N	**7599**	LNA252P	**7659**	ONF659R	**7719**	RJA719R	**7779**	UNA779S
7540	HNB30N	**7600**	LJA600P	**7660**	ONF660R	**7720**	RJA720R	**7780**	UNA780S
7541	HNB31N	**7601**	LJA601P	**7661**	ONF661R	**7721**	RJA721R	**7781**	UNA781S
7542	HNB32N	**7602**	LJA602P	**7662**	ONF662R	**7722**	RJA722R	**7782**	UNA782S
7543	HNB33N	**7603**	LJA603P	**7663**	ONF663R	**7723**	RJA723R	**7783**	UNA783S
7544	HNB34N	**7604**	LJA604P	**7664**	ONF664R	**7724**	RJA724R	**7784**	UNA784S
7545	HNB35N	**7605**	LJA605P	**7665**	ONF665R	**7725**	RJA725R	**7785**	UNA785S
7546	HNB36N	**7606**	LJA606P	**7666**	ONF666R	**7726**	RJA726R	**7786**	UNA786S
7547	HNB37N	**7607**	LJA607P	**7667**	ONF667R	**7727**	RJA727R	**7787**	UNA787S
7548	HNB38N	**7608**	LJA608P	**7668**	ONF668R	**7728**	RJA728R	**7788**	UNA788S
7549	HNB39N	**7609**	LJA609P	**7669**	ONF669R	**7729**	RJA729R	**7789**	UNA789S
7550	HNB40N	**7610**	LJA610P	**7670**	ONF670R	**7730**	RJA730R	**7790**	UNA790S
7551	HNB41N	**7611**	LJA611P	**7671**	ONF671R	**7731**	SRJ731R	**7791**	UNA791S
7552	HNB42N	**7612**	LJA612P	**7672**	ONF672R	**7732**	SRJ732R	**7792**	UNA792S
7553	HNB43N	**7613**	LJA613P	**7673**	ONF673R	**7733**	SRJ733R	**7793**	UNA793S
7554	HNB44N	**7614**	LJA614P	**7674**	ONF674R	**7734**	SRJ734R	**7794**	UNA794S
7555	HNB45N	**7615**	LJA615P	**7675**	ONF675R	**7735**	SRJ735R	**7795**	UNA795S
7556	HJA112N	**7616**	LJA616P	**7676**	ONF676R	**7736**	SRJ736R	**7796**	UNA796S
7557	HJA113N	**7617**	LJA617P	**7677**	ONF677R	**7737**	SRJ737R	**7797**	UNA797S
7558	HJA114N	**7618**	LJA618P	**7678**	ONF678R	**7738**	SRJ738R	**7798**	UNA798S
7559	HJA115N	**7619**	LJA619P	**7679**	ONF679R	**7739**	SRJ739R	**7799**	UNA799S
7560	JND984N	**7620**	LJA620P	**7680**	ONF680R	**7740**	SRJ740R	**7800**	UNA800S

7801–7960

Chassis Leyland Atlantean AN68A/1R
Bodywork Park Royal H43/32F Mark 1a Standard

Built 1977-9
Number in Stock 160

7801	RJA801R	7833	UNA833S	7865	UNA865S	7897	WVM897S	7929	ANC929T
7802	RJA802R	7834	UNA834S	7866	UNA866S	7898	WVM898S	7930	ANC930T
7803	RJA803R	7835	UNA835S	7867	UNA867S	7899	WVM899S	7931	ANC931T
7804	RJA804R	7836	UNA836S	7868	UNA868S	7900	WVM900S	7932	ANC932T
7805	RJA805R	7837	UNA837S	7869	UNA869S	7901	WVM901S	7933	BNC933T
7806	RJA806R	7838	UNA838S	7870	UNA870S	7902	WVM902S	7934	BNC934T
7807	RJA807R	7839	UNA839S	7871	UNA871S	7903	ANC903T	7935	BNC935T
7808	RJA808R	7840	UNA840S	7872	UNA872S	7904	ANC904T	7936	BNC936T
7809	RJA809R	7841	UNA841S	7873	WVM873S	7905	ANC905T	7937	BNC937T
7810	RJA810R	7842	UNA842S	7874	WVM874S	7906	ANC906T	7938	BNC938T
7811	RJA811R	7843	UNA843S	7875	WVM875S	7907	ANC907T	7939	BNC939T
7812	RJA812R	7844	UNA844S	7876	WVM876S	7908	ANC908T	7940	BNC940T
7813	RJA813R	7845	UNA845S	7877	WVM877S	7909	ANC909T	7941	BNC941T
7814	RJA814R	7846	UNA846S	7878	WVM878S	7910	ANC910T	7942	BNC942T
7815	RJA815R	7847	UNA847S	7879	WVM879S	7911	ANC911T	7943	BNC943T
7816	RJA816R	7848	UNA848S	7880	WVM880S	7912	ANC912T	7944	BNC944T
7817	UNA817S	7849	UNA849S	7881	WVM881S	7913	ANC913T	7945	BNC945T
7818	UNA818S	7850	UNA850S	7882	WVM882S	7914	ANC914T	7946	BNC946T
7819	UNA819S	7851	UNA851S	7883	WVM883S	7915	ANC915T	7947	BNC947T
7820	UNA820S	7852	UNA852S	7884	WVM884S	7916	ANC916T	7948	BNC948T
7821	UNA821S	7853	UNA853S	7885	WVM885S	7917	ANC917T	7949	BNC949T
7822	UNA822S	7854	UNA854S	7886	WVM886S	7918	ANC918T	7950	BNC950T
7823	UNA823S	7855	UNA855S	7887	WVM887S	7919	ANC919T	7951	BNC951T
7824	UNA824S	7856	UNA856S	7888	WVM888S	7920	ANC920T	7952	BNC952T
7825	UNA825S	7857	UNA857S	7889	WVM889S	7921	ANC921T	7953	BNC953T
7826	UNA826S	7858	UNA858S	7890	WVM890S	7922	ANC922T	7954	BNC954T
7827	UNA827S	7859	UNA859S	7891	WVM891S	7923	ANC923T	7955	BNC955T
7828	UNA828S	7860	UNA860S	7892	WVM892S	7924	ANC924T	7956	BNC956T
7829	UNA829S	7861	UNA861S	7893	WVM893S	7925	ANC925T	7957	BNC957T
7830	UNA830S	7862	UNA862S	7894	WVM894S	7926	ANC926T	7958	BNC958T
7831	UNA831S	7863	UNA863S	7895	WVM895S	7927	ANC927T	7959	BNC959T
7832	UNA832S	7864	UNA864S	7896	WVM896S	7928	ANC928T	7960	BNC960T

8001–8150

Chassis Leyland Fleetline FE30GR
Bodywork Northern Counties H43/32F Mark 1a Standard

Built 1978-80
Number in Stock 150

8001	XBU1S	8031	ANA31T	8061	BVR61T	8091	BVR91T	8121	HDB121V
8002	XBU2S	8032	ANA32T	8062	BVR62T	8092	BVR92T	8122	HDB122V
8003	XBU3S	8033	ANA33T	8063	BVR63T	8093	BVR93T	8123	HDB123V
8004	XBU4S	8034	ANA34T	8064	BVR64T	8094	BVR94T	8124	HDB124V
8005	XBU5S	8035	ANA35T	8065	BVR65T	8095	BVR95T	8125	HDB125V
8006	XBU6S	8036	ANA36T	8066	BVR66T	8096	BVR96T	8126	KDB126V
8007	XBU7S	8037	ANA37T	8067	BVR67T	8097	BVR97T	8127	KDB127V
8008	XBU8S	8038	ANA38T	8068	BVR68T	8098	BVR98T	8128	KDB128V
8009	XBU9S	8039	ANA39T	8069	BVR69T	8099	BVR99T	8129	KDB129V
8010	XBU10S	8040	ANA40T	8070	BVR70T	8100	BVR100T	8130	KDB130V
8011	XBU11S	8041	ANA41T	8071	BVR71T	8101	HDB101V	8131	KDB131V
8012	XBU12S	8042	ANA42T	8072	BVR72T	8102	HDB102V	8132	KDB132V
8013	XBU13S	8043	ANA43T	8073	BVR73T	8103	HDB103V	8133	KDB133V
8014	XBU14S	8044	ANA44T	8074	BVR74T	8104	HDB104V	8134	KDB134V
8015	XBU15S	8045	ANA45T	8075	BVR75T	8105	HDB105V	8135	KDB135V
8016	XBU16S	8046	ANA46T	8076	BVR76T	8106	HDB106V	8136	KDB136V
8017	XBU17S	8047	ANA47T	8077	BVR77T	8107	HDB107V	8137	KDB137V
8018	XBU18S	8048	ANA48T	8078	BVR78T	8108	HDB108V	8138	KDB138V
8019	XBU19S	8049	ANA49T	8079	BVR79T	8109	HDB109V	8139	KDB139V
8020	XBU20S	8050	ANA50T	8080	BVR80T	8110	HDB110V	8140	KDB140V
8021	ANA21T	8051	BVR51T	8081	BVR81T	8111	HDB111V	8141	GNF16V
8022	ANA22T	8052	BVR52T	8082	BVR82T	8112	HDB112V	8142	GNF17V
8023	ANA23T	8053	BVR53T	8083	BVR83T	8113	HDB113V	8143	MNC486W
8024	ANA24T	8054	BVR54T	8084	BVR84T	8114	HDB114V	8144	MNC487W
8025	ANA25T	8055	BVR55T	8085	BVR85T	8115	HDB115V	8145	MNC488W
8026	ANA26T	8056	BVR56T	8086	BVR86T	8116	HDB116V	8146	MNC489W
8027	ANA27T	8057	BVR57T	8087	BVR87T	8117	HDB117V	8147	MNC490W
8028	ANA28T	8058	BVR58T	8088	BVR88T	8118	HDB118V	8148	MNC491W
8029	ANA29T	8059	BVR59T	8089	BVR89T	8119	HDB119V	8149	MNC492W
8030	ANA30T	8060	BVR60T	8090	BVR90T	8120	HDB120V	8150	MNC493W

8151–8400

Chassis Leyland Atlantean AN68A/1R
Bodywork Northern Counties H43/32F Mark 1a Standard
Built 1978-81
Number in Stock 250

8151	VBA151S	**8201**	XRJ201S	**8251**	FVR251V	**8301**	KDB301V	**8351**	ORJ351W
8152	VBA152S	**8202**	XRJ202S	**8252**	FVR252V	**8302**	KDB302V	**8352**	ORJ352W
8153	VBA153S	**8203**a	XRJ203S	**8253**	FVR253V	**8303**	KDB303V	**8353**	ORJ353W
8154	VBA154S	**8204**	XRJ204S	**8254**	FVR254V	**8304**	MNC504W	**8354**	ORJ354W
8155	VBA155S	**8205**	XRJ205S	**8255**	FVR255V	**8305**	MNC505W	**8355**	ORJ355W
8156	VBA156S	**8206**	XRJ206S	**8256**	FVR256V	**8306**	MNC506W	**8356**	ORJ356W
8157	VBA157S	**8207**	ANA207T	**8257**	FVR257V	**8307**	MNC507W	**8357**	ORJ357W
8158	VBA158S	**8208**	ANA208T	**8258**	FVR258V	**8308**	MNC508W	**8358**	ORJ358W
8159	VBA159S	**8209**	ANA209T	**8259**	FVR259V	**8309**	MNC509W	**8359**	ORJ359W
8160	VBA160S	**8210**	ANA210T	**8260**	FVR260V	**8310**	MNC510W	**8360**	ORJ360W
8161	VBA161S	**8211**	ANA211T	**8261**	FVR261V	**8311**	MNC511W	**8361**	ORJ361W
8162	VBA162S	**8212**	ANA212T	**8262**	FVR262V	**8312**	MNC512W	**8362**	ORJ362W
8163	VBA163S	**8213**	ANA213T	**8263**	FVR263V	**8313**	MNC513W	**8363**	ORJ363W
8164	VBA164S	**8214**	ANA214T	**8264**	FVR264V	**8314**	MNC514W	**8364**	ORJ364W
8165	VBA165S	**8215**	ANA215T	**8265**	FVR265V	**8315**	MNC515W	**8365**	ORJ365W
8166	VBA166S	**8216**	ANA216T	**8266**	FVR266V	**8316**	MNC516W	**8366**	ORJ366W
8167	VBA167S	**8217**	ANA217T	**8267**	FVR267V	**8317**	MNC517W	**8367**	ORJ367W
8168	VBA168S	**8218**	ANA218T	**8268**	FVR268V	**8318**	MNC518W	**8368**	ORJ368W
8169	VBA169S	**8219**	ANA219T	**8269**	FVR269V	**8319**	MNC519W	**8369**	ORJ369W
8170	VBA170S	**8220**	ANA220T	**8270**	FVR270V	**8320**	MNC520W	**8370**	ORJ370W
8171	VBA171S	**8221**	ANA221T	**8271**	FVR271V	**8321**	MNC521W	**8371**	ORJ371W
8172	VBA172S	**8222**	ANA222T	**8272**	FVR272V	**8322**	MNC522W	**8372**	ORJ372W
8173	VBA173S	**8223**	ANA223T	**8273**	FVR273V	**8323**	MNC523W	**8373**	ORJ373W
8174	VBA174S	**8224**	ANA224T	**8274**	FVR274V	**8324**	MNC524W	**8374**	ORJ374W
8175	VBA175S	**8225**	ANA225T	**8275**	FVR275V	**8325**	MNC525W	**8375**	ORJ375W
8176	VBA176S	**8226**	ANA226T	**8276**	FVR276V	**8326**	MNC526W	**8376**	ORJ376W
8177	VBA177S	**8227**	ANA227T	**8277**	FVR277V	**8327**	MNC527W	**8377**	ORJ377W
8178	VBA178S	**8228**	ANA228T	**8278**	FVR278V	**8328**	MNC528W	**8378**	ORJ378W
8179	VBA179S	**8229**	ANA229T	**8279**	FVR279V	**8329**	MNC529W	**8379**	ORJ379W
8180	VBA180S	**8230**	ANA230T	**8280**	FVR280V	**8330**	MNC530W	**8380**	ORJ380W
8181	VBA181S	**8231**	ANA231T	**8281**	FVR281V	**8331**	MNC531W	**8381**	ORJ381W
8182	VBA182S	**8232**	ANA232T	**8282**	FVR282V	**8332**	MNC532W	**8382**	ORJ382W
8183	VBA183S	**8233**	ANA233T	**8283**	FVR283V	**8333**	MNC533W	**8383**d	ORJ383W
8184	VBA184S	**8234**	ANA234T	**8284**	FVR284V	**8334**	MNC534W	**8384**	ORJ384W
8185	VBA185S	**8235**	ANA235T	**8285**	FVR285V	**8335**	MNC535W	**8385**	ORJ385W
8186	VBA186S	**8236**b	ANA236T	**8286**	FVR286V	**8336**	MNC536W	**8386**	ORJ386W
8187	VBA187S	**8237**	ANA237T	**8287**	FVR287V	**8337**	MNC537W	**8387**	ORJ387W
8188	VBA188S	**8238**	ANA238T	**8288**	FVR288V	**8338**	MNC538W	**8388**	ORJ388W
8189	VBA189S	**8239**	ANA239T	**8289**	FVR289V	**8339**	MNC539W	**8389**	ORJ389W
8190	VBA190S	**8240**	FVR240V	**8290**	FVR290V	**8340**	MNC540W	**8390**	ORJ390W
8191	VBA191S	**8241**	ANA241T	**8291**	FVR291V	**8341**	MNC541W	**8391**	ORJ391W
8192	VBA192S	**8242**	FVR242V	**8292**c	FVR292V	**8342**	MNC542W	**8392**	ORJ392W
8193	VBA193S	**8243**	FVR243V	**8293**	FVR293V	**8343**	MNC543W	**8393**	ORJ393W
8194	VBA194S	**8244**	FVR244V	**8294**	FVR294V	**8344**	MNC544W	**8394**	ORJ394W
8195	VBA195S	**8245**	FVR245V	**8295**	FVR295V	**8345**	MNC545W	**8395**	ORJ395W
8196	VBA196S	**8246**	FVR246V	**8296**	FVR296V	**8346**	MNC546W	**8396**	ORJ396W
8197	VBA197S	**8247**	FVR247V	**8297**	FVR297V	**8347**	MNC547W	**8397**	ORJ397W
8198	VBA198S	**8248**	FVR248V	**8298**	FVR298V	**8348**	MNC548W	**8398**	ORJ398W
8199	VBA199S	**8249**	FVR249V	**8299**	FVR299V	**8349**	MNC549W	**8399**	ORJ399W
8200	VBA200S	**8250**	FVR250V	**8300**	FVR300V	**8350**	MNC550W	**8400**	ORJ400W

a Advertisement bus for Quick's (Ford dealers)
b Advertisement bus for Phoenix Assurance
c Advertisement bus for Johnstone's Paints
d Advertisement bus for Rhyl Sun Centre

8401–8525

Chassis Leyland Atlantean AN68A/1R (8425/48/9/55/6/60-6/8-72/4-8/80/1/3-5/90/3/4/500-25: AN68B/1R)
Bodywork Northern Counties H43/32F
8401-32/4-6/9-42 Mark 1a Standard
8433/7/8/43-525 Light alloy Standard

Built 1981/2
Number in Stock 125

8401	MRJ401W	**8426**	SND426X	**8451**	SND451X	**8476**	SND476X	**8501**	SND501X
8402	MRJ402W	**8427**	SND427X	**8452**	SND452X	**8477**	SND477X	**8502**	SND502X
8403	MRJ403W	**8428**	SND428X	**8453**	SND453X	**8478**	SND478X	**8503**	SND503X
8404	MRJ404W	**8429**	SND429X	**8454**	SND454X	**8479**	SND479X	**8504**	SND504X
8405	MRJ405W	**8430**	SND430X	**8455**	SND455X	**8480**	SND480X	**8505**	SND505X
8406	MRJ406W	**8431**	SND431X	**8456**	SND456X	**8481**	SND481X	**8506**	SND506X
8407	MRJ407W	**8432**	SND432X	**8457**	SND457X	**8482**	SND482X	**8507**	SND507X
8408	MRJ408W	**8433**	SND433X	**8458**	SND458X	**8483**	SND483X	**8508**	SND508X
8409	MRJ409W	**8434**	SND434X	**8459**	SND459X	**8484**	SND484X	**8509**	SND509X
8410	MRJ410W	**8435**	SND435X	**8460**	SND460X	**8485**	SND485X	**8510**	SND510X
8411	MRJ411W	**8436**	SND436X	**8461**	SND461X	**8486**	SND486X	**8511**	SND511X
8412	SND412X	**8437**	SND437X	**8462**	SND462X	**8487**	SND487X	**8512**	SND512X
8413	SND413X	**8438**	SND438X	**8463**	SND463X	**8488**	SND488X	**8513**	SND513X
8414	SND414X	**8439**	SND439X	**8464**	SND464X	**8489**	SND489X	**8514**	SND514X
8415	SND415X	**8440**	SND440X	**8465**	SND465X	**8490**	SND490X	**8515**	SND515X
8416	SND416X	**8441**	SND441X	**8466**	SND466X	**8491**	SND491X	**8516**	SND516X
8417	SND417X	**8442**	SND442X	**8467**	SND467X	**8492**	SND492X	**8517**	SND517X
8418	SND418X	**8443**	SND443X	**8468**	SND468X	**8493**	SND493X	**8518**	SND518X
8419	SND419X	**8444**	SND444X	**8469**	SND469X	**8494**	SND494X	**8519**	SND519X
8420	SND420X	**8445**	SND445X	**8470**	SND470X	**8495**	SND495X	**8520**	SND520X
8421	SND421X	**8446**	SND446X	**8471**	SND471X	**8496**	SND496X	**8521**a	SND521X
8422	SND422X	**8447**	SND447X	**8472**	SND472X	**8497**	SND497X	**8522**	SND522X
8423	SND423X	**8448**	SND448X	**8473**	SND473X	**8498**	SND498X	**8523**	SND523X
8424	SND424X	**8449**	SND449X	**8474**	SND474X	**8499**	SND499X	**8524**	SND524X
8425	SND425X	**8450**	SND450X	**8475**	SND475X	**8500**	SND500X	**8525**	SND525X

a Advertisement bus for Looker's (Austin Rover dealers)

8526–8700

Chassis Leyland Atlantean AN68D/1R
Bodywork Northern Counties H43/32F Light alloy Standard

Built 1982/3
Number in Stock 105

8526	SND526X	**8561**	ANA561Y	**8596**	ANA596Y	**8631**	ANA631Y	**8666**	
8527	SND527X	**8562**	ANA562Y	**8597**	ANA597Y	**8632**		**8667**	
8528	SND528X	**8563**	ANA563Y	**8598**	ANA598Y	**8633**		**8668**	
8529	SND529X	**8564**	ANA564Y	**8599**	ANA599Y	**8634**		**8669**	
8530	SND530X	**8565**	ANA565Y	**8600**	ANA600Y	**8635**		**8670**	
8531	ANA531Y	**8566**	ANA566Y	**8601**	ANA601Y	**8636**		**8671**	
8532	ANA532Y	**8567**	ANA567Y	**8602**	ANA602Y	**8637**		**8672**	
8533	ANA533Y	**8568**	ANA568Y	**8603**	ANA603Y	**8638**		**8673**	
8534	ANA534Y	**8569**	ANA569Y	**8604**	ANA604Y	**8639**		**8674**	
8535	ANA535Y	**8570**	ANA570Y	**8605**	ANA605Y	**8640**		**8675**	
8536	ANA536Y	**8571**	ANA571Y	**8606**	ANA606Y	**8641**		**8676**	
8537	ANA537Y	**8572**	ANA572Y	**8607**	ANA607Y	**8642**		**8677**	
8538	ANA538Y	**8573**	ANA573Y	**8608**	ANA608Y	**8643**		**8678**	
8539	ANA539Y	**8574**	ANA574Y	**8609**	ANA609Y	**8644**		**8679**	
8540	ANA540Y	**8575**	ANA575Y	**8610**	ANA610Y	**8645**		**8680**	
8541	ANA541Y	**8576**	ANA576Y	**8611**	ANA611Y	**8646**		**8681**	
8542	ANA542Y	**8577**	ANA577Y	**8612**	ANA612Y	**8647**		**8682**	
8543	ANA543Y	**8578**	ANA578Y	**8613**	ANA613Y	**8648**		**8683**	
8544	ANA544Y	**8579**	ANA579Y	**8614**	ANA614Y	**8649**		**8684**	
8545	ANA545Y	**8580**	ANA580Y	**8615**	ANA615Y	**8650**		**8685**	
8546	ANA546Y	**8581**a	ANA581Y	**8616**	ANA616Y	**8651**		**8686**	
8547	ANA547Y	**8582**a	ANA582Y	**8617**	ANA617Y	**8652**		**8687**	
8548	ANA548Y	**8583**	ANA583Y	**8618**	ANA618Y	**8653**		**8688**	
8549	ANA549Y	**8584**a	ANA584Y	**8619**	ANA619Y	**8654**		**8689**	
8550	ANA550Y	**8585**a	ANA585Y	**8620**	ANA620Y	**8655**		**8690**	
8551	ANA551Y	**8586**	ANA586Y	**8621**	ANA621Y	**8656**		**8691**	
8552	ANA552Y	**8587**	ANA587Y	**8622**	ANA622Y	**8657**		**8692**	
8553	ANA553Y	**8588**	ANA588Y	**8623**	ANA623Y	**8658**		**8693**	
8554	ANA554Y	**8589**	ANA589Y	**8624**	ANA624Y	**8659**		**8694**	
8555	ANA555Y	**8590**	ANA590Y	**8625**	ANA625Y	**8660**		**8695**	
8556	ANA556Y	**8591**	ANA591Y	**8626**	ANA626Y	**8661**		**8696**	
8557	ANA557Y	**8592**	ANA592Y	**8627**	ANA627Y	**8662**		**8697**	
8558	ANA558Y	**8593**	ANA593Y	**8628**	ANA628Y	**8663**		**8698**	
8559	ANA559Y	**8594**	ANA594Y	**8629**	ANA629Y	**8664**		**8699**	
8560	ANA560Y	**8595**	ANA595Y	**8630**		**8665**		**8700**	

a Advertisement bus for Bus & Coach Council

Batch will continue to 8825

MERSEYSIDE TRANSPORT

The Merseyside Passenger Transport Executive was set up in December 1969 when the municipal fleets of Liverpool, Birkenhead and Wallasey were taken over. Following local government reorganisation the operations of St Helens and Southport were acquired on 1st April 1974.

Development of public transport proceeded along familiar lines with horse bus operation from the mid 19th century being followed by horse trams later. The first of the latter was a short-lived experiment in 1859 in Liverpool which ran over the railway lines in the docks. In 1860 Britain's first street horse tramway began in Birkenhead, using a stepped rail with the outer edge of the rail projecting about $\frac{5}{8}$ inch above the road surface. There were many complaints about this arrangement and the rails were replaced by the more normal grooved variety. Horse trams were introduced again in Liverpool in 1869, Southport in 1873, Wallasey in 1879 and St Helens in 1881. The St Helens ones were the shortest lived since they were replaced by steam trams in 1890, this being the only permanent use of this form of traction on Merseyside.

By the turn of the century most of the track was owned by the local authorities but leased for operation to private companies. Only Liverpool (in 1897) and Wallasey (in 1901) took over operation of horse cars direct. The last horse trams ran in Birkenhead in 1901, Southport and Wallasey in 1902 and Liverpool in 1903. The last steam trams ran in St Helens in 1901.

When it came to electrification a good deal of civic pride was involved and apart from St Helens and part of Southport, the new electric trams were operated by the municipalities. Liverpool commenced in 1898 followed by Southport Corporation in 1900, Birkenhead in 1901 and Wallasey in 1902. The remainder of the Southport system running into Birkdale was operated by a BET subsidiary, Southport Tramways Company and this was electrified in 1901 and finally purchased by Southport Corporation on 1st January 1918. St Helens was the only authority to lease back the electrified tramways to a private operator, the New St Helens and District Tramways Company. Electrification commenced in 1899 and the company was purchased by the corporation in 1919.

The first motor buses appeared in Liverpool in January 1911 and were operated as feeders to the tramway system, a feature which was due to remain until the late 1940s in this city. It was after the Great War in 1919 that Birkenhead started to run buses, followed by Wallasey in 1920, St Helens in 1921 and Southport in 1924. Initially, as in Liverpool, they were used as feeders but as cars and tracks began to wear out the more lightly-used lines were converted to bus operation. However, the development of the bus was rapid and with the advent of the double decker in the form of the Leyland Titan and AEC Regent it became practical to replace the heaviest tram services. Thus trams bowed out to the bus, the last operating in Wallasey in 1933, Southport in 1934 and Birkenhead in 1937.

However, St Helens chose a different mode to replace its trams and introduced trolleybuses, which progressively took over the system until the last tram ran in April 1936. In addition to the local services the St Helens trolleybuses worked the long route to Atherton jointly with the South Lancs Transport Company until abandonment in 1956. The last of the local routes ran in June 1958.

The biggest system of all, in Liverpool, went in the reverse direction and new tramway extensions were opened in the 1930s and early 1940s on reserved track. A sizeable fleet of new streamlined trams was also built to operate these new routes and replace older stock. It was not until 1945 that Liverpool City Council decided to substitute buses and the conversion period lasted from 1948 to September 1957.

Liverpool and St Helens were both involved in joint operations with the surrounding company operators, and since its formation the PTE has reached agreements on the levels of fares and services with Crosville Motor Services, Ribble Motor Services and Lancashire United Transport (now Greater Manchester PTE).

Vehicle policy of the former municipal operators was not as cohesive as that in the Greater Manchester area, for whilst all of them, apart from Liverpool, purchased local Leyland products in the tram replacement era, other makes also were used including locally produced Vulcan double deckers in Southport. Liverpool preferred AEC Regents in the 1930s and some were also to be found in Wallasey. A few Daimlers were also used by the two Wirral operators. During the second world war utility Guys and Bristols went into service with Liverpool and St Helens, Guys to Birkenhead and a large batch of Daimlers to Southport.

In post-war years Leylands went to all operators, AECs to Liverpool and St Helens, Crossleys to Liverpool and Southport, Daimlers to Liverpool and Birkenhead and Guys to Birkenhead. When the rear-engined double decker came into fashion the Leyland Atlantean was chosen by all the operators apart from St Helens, who favoured single-deck AEC Swifts, and a solitary batch of Daimler Fleetlines supplied to Birkenhead.

On first formation, the PTE operated two separate divisions and unusually had two different liveries. Liverpool operations remained green and cream but the Wirral vehicles were in blue and cream. Initially in 1974 the Southport and St Helens based vehicles retained red and cream but from October 1974 all these local variations gave way to the now standard Verona Green and cream which is supplemented on some vehicles by brown skirts and window surrounds, the latter being self-coloured plastic.

To a large extent the PTE has carried on from Liverpool Corporation in vehicle policy, purchasing a large fleet of Leyland Atlanteans supplemented by Bristol VRs and REs. Scania/MCW Metropolitans have been purchased in single- and double-deck form and a batch of Daimler Fleetlines for the Wirral operations. There has also been a sizeable intake of Leyland Nationals and more recently small evaluation batches of Metrobuses, Olympians, Dominators and Volvo Ailsas have been purchased.

Garages are situated at Birkenhead (Laird Street), Liverpool (Edge Lane, Garston, Gillmoss, Green Lane, Litherland, Prince Alfred Road, Speke and Walton), St Helens (Jackson Street), Southport (Canning Road) and Wallasey (Seaview Road).

Merseyside PTE still runs a considerable number of ex-St Helens AEC Swifts, all with Marshall bodies. No. 247, seen in front of the Library and Art Gallery in St Helens, belongs to the 1971 delivery. Virtually all operations in St Helens are single-deck. D.D. Kirk

Two Leyland 550FG midibuses with Alexander (Belfast) bodies were purchased for use in Wallasey in 1974. No. 331 has subsequently been withdrawn, but sister bus 332, seen at Seaview Road, is still in stock. L.J. Long

Merseyside has purchased quite a number of small batches of vehicles for evaluation purposes since 1979. They have been numbered in an 00xx series. No. 0020 was delivered in 1979 and is a Metro-Cammell Weymann Metrobus with mark 1 body. The batch of five has two mechanical specifications, two being DR101s with Gardner 6LXB engines, the other three being DR103s with Rolls-Royce engines. All have hydraulic brakes. No. 0020 is a DR101 and is seen at Gilmoss garage in March 1983. L.J. Long

No. 0024 is the first of five Dennis Dominators (DD120B) with Willowbrook bodies supplied in 1980. The body style is similar to that fitted to Atlanteans 1843-72 delivered in 1980/1, apart from the provision of a front air intake for the radiator and the absence of a 'bustle' at the rear. R.L. Wilson

Two batches of five Bristol built Leyland Olympian ONTL11/1Rs with Eastern Coachworks bodies have been purchased and five more are on order. 0032 is one of the first batch delivered in 1981 and is seen here at Pier Head, Liverpool. An electronic indicator display is fitted. L.J. Long

0036 is one of a pair of Dennis Dominator DDA145s with Alexander R type bodies delivered in 1982. The style of body is very different from the standard AL type built in considerable numbers on Atlantean chassis. D. Savage

Looking very similar to 0036 is 0055, but it is based on the front engined Volvo Ailsa B55-10 chassis. It is seen leaving Heswall Bus Station. The T suffix on the side fleet number plate indicates that the bus is fitted with a tachograph. R.L. Wilson

Merseyside is one of a number of operators to have specified Alexander bodies on MCW Metrobus chassis. Ten are currently in stock, two of Rolls-Royce engined DR104 type, the remainder of Gardner engined DR102 type. These vehicles differ from the original Metrobuses in having air brakes. No. 0060 is a DR102 of 1982 and is seen in Lime Street, Liverpool on its way to Pier Head. D.D. Kirk

Merseyside maintains a fleet of open toppers for use at the well-known seaside resort of Southport. They are in the former Southport Corporation red and cream livery and carry a radiator board to further identify that they are Merseyside PTE buses. No. 0653 is a 1965 Weymann bodied Leyland Titan PD2/40 and was ex-Southport 53 in 1974. R.L. Wilson

Only two of the once-numerous Leyland Panthers taken over from Southport Corporation in 1974 now remain in service. Marshall-bodied 0673, a PSUR1A/1R, new in 1971, is seen in Southport in 1983. D. Savage

The only former Liverpool City Transport bus to remain in public service is 0677: It was new in 1964 as L677, passing to the PTE in 1969. It is a Leyland Atlantean PDR1/1 and its Metro-Cammell body was rebuilt to open top in 1975. It was renumbered in 1982. Livery is Southport red/cream in common with 0653. R.L. Wilson

Ten 1973 Leyland Atlantean AN68s with Alexander dual-door AL type bodies were acquired from Southport Corporation in 1974. No. 0682 (ex-82) is seen in the latest Merseyside livery in Lord Street, Southport. R.L. Wilson

No. 1219 is one of 125 dual doorway Alexander bodied Leyland Atlantean PDR2s delivered between 1969 and 1972. This bus was new in 1971 and is seen in Lime Street, Liverpool. A.E. Hall

In 1972/3, 160 Leyland Atlanteans with Alexander AL type single-doorway bodies were delivered. The first 60 had PDR1A/1 chassis, the remainder being of the new AN68/1R type. No. 1299 of the latter batch was delivered in 1972 and is seen in Denby Square. R.L. Wilson

Delivered in 1978, Leyland Atlantean AN68A/1 No. 1777 carries a Metro-Cammell Weymann body, one of a batch of 45. It is seen at Speke. D. Savage

No. 1789, of the same batch, was one of six buses painted into special historic liveries in 1979 as part of the 50th anniversary celebrations of Edge Lane works, Liverpool. When photographed in April 1983, it still carried a modified form of the Wallasey Corporation livery it received, but the other five vehicles have now been repainted to standard. L.J. Bowles

East Lancashire bodied 152 of Merseyside's Leyland Atlantean AN68s between 1973 and 1980. One of the last to be placed in service in 1980 was No. 1830 seen at Pier Head. R.L. Wilson

Between 1980 and 1982 Willowbrook bodied thirty Leyland Atlantean AN68B/1Rs of a design not unlike that supplied on Bristol VRT chassis to several NBC companies. No. 1845 was new in 1980. R.L. Wilson

A return to Alexander AL type bodywork was made on 119 vehicles delivered in 1981/2. No 1902, new in 1981, shows how these bodies on Leyland Atlantean AN68 chassis have a completely flat body panel beneath the windscreen. The vehicle is seen at West Kirby on a special golf tournament service. A further fifteen AL type bodied Atlanteans are on order. R.L. Wilson

It had been Liverpool's policy to buy a proportion of its buses from Bristol, and Merseyside continued this dual-sourcing practice. Fifty-nine of the unusual VRT/LH6LX chassis were purchased in 1970/1 and received East Lancashire dual-doorway bodywork. There was to have been a sixtieth but this vehicle was destroyed in a fire at the bodybuilders. The chassis were unusual in having a high frame (indicated by the H in the designation) to accommodate the so-called Liverpool entrance design which had an extra step, but therefore reduced the height of the individual risers. A nominal overall length of 33 feet enabled 80 seated passengers to be carried, which with 21 standees gave a total capacity of 101, surely one of the highest in Britain. No. 2037 of 1970, seen here at Pier Head, Liverpool in March 1982 was withdrawn in August of that year despite the good condition evident in the photograph. Four of the type remained in passenger service at the time of writing. R.L. Wilson

Ten Bristol RESL6Ls with Eastern Coachworks bodies were bought in 1971, of which three remain in service. Amongst these is 2093 seen outside Liverpool Central Station. R.L. Wilson

The next fifty Bristol VRTs were of the more conventional SL/6LX variant with shorter chassis (S) and low frame (L). Once again East Lancashire bodywork was fitted but with a single doorway. No. 2139 of 1975 is seen turning into Lime Street opposite the station. M.S. Stokes

Five Bristol LHS6L with Eastern Coachworks bodies were acquired from West Yorkshire PTE in 1980 to work the Toxteth community service. Four remain in service, including 2156 seen in Elliot Street, Liverpool. Ten Duple Dominant bodied Dennis Lancets are on order and will probably replace the remaining LHSs. D. Savage

In 1973 a batch of fifty Metro-Cammell Weymann bodied Daimler Fleetline CRG6LXBs was purchased for operation in the Wirral Division. Overchurch terminus is the setting for this photograph of 3027. R.L. Wilson

A further variation of manufacturer in 1972 came with the introduction of the Scania BR111MH single decker with Metro-Cammell Weymann body, twenty being purchased. No. 4016 is seen at Prince Alfred Road. L.J. Long

Sixty of the double-deck Metropolitans with Scania BR111DH chassis and Metro-Cammell Weymann bodies were bought in 1974/5. No. 4050 of 1974 is seen at Liverpool Pier Head. L.J. Long

Merseyside has built up a large fleet of Leyland Nationals of various types. No. 6035 is a 1979 Leyland National 2 of type NL116L11/1R and together with the other six of the batch is unusual in not having the rear roof-mounted heating/ventilating pod. The bus is seen in Ainsdale. R.L. Wilson

Southport Corporation purchased eight Leyland Nationals of type 1151/2R in 1974, just before Merseyside took over. No. 6045 (Southport 4) is seen in Lord Street, Southport still in the two door configuration. The batch has now been rebuilt to single door, each vehicle gaining three extra seats (to a capacity of 49) as a result. R.L. Wilson

Representing the 94 Leyland National 2s of the NL116AL11/1R type is 6121 of 1980. This view is particularly interesting since it shows the bus alongside Merseyside PTE's M.V. 'Overchurch' at Trafford Wharf, Stretford, Manchester Docks. This possibly unique shot of a PTE bus and boat together came about because of the need to change over the crew of the boat. R.L. Wilson

Merseyside has three dual-purpose Leyland National 11351A/1Rs dating from 1978. The first of these, 7000, is seen in Southport on the free Park and Ride service between the railway station and the town centre. D. Savage

Four dual-purpose Leyland National 2s of type NL116AL11/1R were bought in 1981. Seen when new at Seaview Road, Wallasey depot is 7006. R.L. Wilson

Operation of full luxury coaches, but with bus grant body specification, began in 1980. No. 7003, a Leyland Leopard PSU3 with Duple Dominant body is seen here in Lord Street, Southport. It was joined in 1981 by similar vehicle 7008. R.L. Wilson

In 1982 the luxury coach fleet was considerably expanded with the addition of twelve Leyland Tiger TRCTL11/2Rs with Duple Dominant coachwork. Numerically the first of the batch, No. 7009 is seen in the coach park of the National Exhibition Centre at Birmingham conveying visitors to the 1982 Motor Show. It is pleasing to see the Tiger emblem displayed prominently on the front panel. M.R. Keeley

In an unusual move early in 1983, ten of these Fleetlines (3011-20) were put on long term loan to Crosville Motor Services. To all intents and purposes the vehicles appear to be Crosville's own since they are licensed and taxed by the company. Seen at Heswall depot are 3016 and 3019, now numbered HDG937 and 939 respectively in the Crosville fleet. R.L. Wilson

MERSEYSIDE TRANSPORT FLEET LIST

61

Chassis Leyland Titan PD2/40
Bodywork Massey H36/30R
Acquired from Birkenhead Corporation (131) in 1969

Built 1966
Number in Stock 1

61t DBG131D

t Training bus

L706–878

Chassis Leyland Atlantean PDR1/1
Bodywork Metro-Cammell H43/35F (L706-812)
Metro-Cammell Weymann H43/28D (L832-878)
Acquired from Liverpool City Transport in 1969
(same numbers)

Built 1965-7
Number in Stock 6

706t	CKF706C	**812**t	FKF812D	**832**t	FKF832E	**837**t	FKF837E	**878**t	FKF878E
806t	FKF806D								

t Training bus

242–286

Chassis AEC Swift MP2R (236/7), 2MP2R (242-59),
3MP2R (260-86)
Bodywork Marshall B44D (242-68), B42D (269-86)
236-77 ex-St Helens Corporation 1974 (same numbers)

Built 1971/72/73/75
Number in Stock 41

242	EDJ242J	**251**	EDJ251J	**263**	JDJ263K	**271**	PDJ271L	**279**	GEM599N
243	EDJ243J	**252**	EDJ252J	**264**	JDJ264K	**272**	PDJ272L	**280**	GEM600N
244	EDJ244J	**253**	EDJ253J	**265**	JDJ265K	**273**	PDJ273L	**281**	GEM601N
245	EDJ245J	**254**	EDJ254J	**266**	JDJ266K	**274**	PDJ274L	**282**	GEM602N
246	EDJ246J	**259**	EDJ255J	**267**	JDJ267K	**275**	PDJ275L	**283**	GEM603N
247	EDJ247J	**260**	JDJ260K	**268**	JDJ268K	**276**	PDJ276L	**284**	GEM604N
248	EDJ248J	**261**	JDJ261K	**269**	PDJ269L	**277**	PDJ277L	**285**	GEM605N
249	EDJ249J	**262**	JDJ262K	**270**	PDJ270L	**278**	GEM598N	**286**	GEM606N
250	EDJ250J								

332

Chassis Leyland 550FG
Bodywork Alexander (Belfast) B22F

Built 1974
Number in Stock 1

332 RKA424N

0019–23

Chassis Metro-Cammell Weymann Metrobus
DR101/13 (0019/20), DR 103/2 (0021-3)
Bodywork Metro-Cammell Weymann H43/30F
0019/20 have Gardner engines
0021-3 have Rolls-Royce engines

Built 1979/80

0019	UKA19V	**0020**	UKA20V	**0021**	UKA21V	**0022**	UKA22V	**0023**	UKA23V

0024–28

Chassis Dennis Dominator DD120B
Bodywork Willowbrook H45/33F

Built 1980
Number in Stock 5

0024	UBG24V	**0025**	UBG25V	**0026**	WWM918W	**0027**	WWM904W	**0028**	WWM919W

0030–34

Chassis Leyland (Bristol) Olympian ONTL11/1R
Bodywork Eastern Coachworks H46/31F

Built 1981
Number in Stock 5

0030	ACM704X	**0031**	ACM705X	**0032**	ACM706X	**0033**	ACM707X	**0034**	ACM708X

0035/36

Chassis Dennis Dominator DDA 145
Bodywork Alexander H45/31F

Built 1982
Number in Stock 2

0035	ACM768X	**0036**	ACM769X

0037–41

Chassis Leyland (Bristol) Olympian ONTL11/1R
Bodywork Eastern Coachworks H46/31F

Built 1982
Number in Stock 5

0037	ACM709X	**0038**	ACM710X	**0039**	ACM711X	**0040**	ACM712X	**0041**	ACM772X

0042/43

Chassis Metro-Cammell Weymann Metrobus DR104/9
Bodywork Alexander H45/31F
Rolls-Royce engines are fitted

Built 1982
Number in Stock 2

0042	ACM770X	**0043**	ACM771X

0046–53

Chassis Dennis Dominator DDA157
Bodywork Alexander H45/33F

Built 1982
Number in Stock 8

0046	CHF346X	**0048**	CHF348X	**0050**	CHF350X	**0052**	CHF352X	**0053**	CHF353X
0047	CHF347X	**0049**	CHF349X	**0051**	CHF351X				

0054/55

Chassis Volvo Ailsa B55-10
Bodywork Alexander H44/35F

Built 1982
Number in Stock 2

0054	DEM821Y	**0055**	DEM822Y

0056–63

Chassis Metro-Cammell Weymann Metrobus DR102/29
Bodywork Alexander H45/31F
Gardner engines are fitted.

Built 1982
Number in Stock 8

0056	EKA156Y	**0058**	DEM758Y	**0060**	DEM760Y	**0062**	DEM762Y	**0063**	DEM763Y
0057	EKA157Y	**0059**	DEM759Y	**0061**	DEM761Y				

0651–54

Chassis Leyland Titan PD2/40
Bodywork Weymann O37/27F
Acquired from Southport Corporation (51/3/4) in 1974

Built 1965
Number in Stock 3

0651	CWM151C	**0653**	CWM153C	**0654**	CWM154C

0658

Chassis Leyland Titan PD2/40
Bodywork Metro-Cammell Weymann H-/16F
Acquired from Southport Corporation (58) in 1974

Built 1967
Number in Stock 1

0658t	GFY58E

t Training bus

0672/0673

Chassis Leyland Panther PSU1A/1R
Bodywork Marshall B43D
Acquired from Southport Corporation (72/3) in 1974

Built 1972
Number in Stock 2

0672	PFY72J	**0673**	PFY73J

0677

Chassis Leyland Atlantean PDR1/1
Bodywork Metro-Cammell O43/34F
Acquired from Liverpool City Transport (L677) in 1969

Built 1974
Number in Stock 1

0677	677KD

0681–0690

Chassis Leyland Atlantean AN68/1R
Bodywork Alexander H45/29D
Acquired from Southport Corporation (81-90) in 1974

Built 1973
Number in Stock 10

0681	VWM81L	**0683**	VWM83L	**0685**	VWM85L	**0687**	VWM87L	**0689**	VWM89L
0682	VWM82L	**0684**	VWM84L	**0686**	VWM86L	**0688**	VWM88L	**0690**	VWM90L

1111–1235

Chassis Leyland Atlantean PDR2/1
Bodywork Alexander H47/32D (1111-75) or
Alexander H49/31D (1178-1235)
1111 ex-Liverpool Corporation in 1969 (same number)

Built 1969-72
Number in Stock 40

1111t	UKA562H	**1204**	XKC831K	**1212**	XKC839K	**1220**	XKC847K	**1228**	XKC855K
1150t	UKA601H	**1205**	XKC832K	**1213**	XKC840K	**1221**	XKC848K	**1229**	XKC856K
1162	XKC789J	**1206**	XKC833K	**1214**	XKC841K	**1222**	XKC849K	**1230**	XKC857K
1174t	XKC801J	**1207**	XKC834K	**1215**	XKC842K	**1223**	XKC850K	**1231**	XKC858K
1181	XKC808K	**1208**	XKC835K	**1216**	XKC843K	**1224**	XKC851K	**1232**	XKC859K
1201	XKC828K	**1209**	XKC836K	**1217**	XKC844K	**1225**	XKC852K	**1233**	XKC860K
1202	XKC829K	**1210**	XKC837K	**1218**	XKC845K	**1226**	XKC853K	**1234**	XKC861K
1203	XKC830K	**1211**	XKC838K	**1219**	XKC846K	**1227**	XKC854K	**1235**	XKC862K

t Training bus

1236–1395

Chassis Leyland Atlantean PDR1A/1 (1236-95)
AN68/1R (1296-1395)
Bodywork Alexander H43/32F

Built 1972/3
Number in Stock 158

1236	BKC236K	**1269**	BKC269K	**1301**	DKC301L	**1333**	DKC333L	**1365**	DKC365L
1237	BKC237K	**1270**	BKC270K	**1302**	DKC302L	**1334**	DKC334L	**1366**	DKC366L
1238	BKC238K	**1271**	BKC271K	**1303**	DKC303L	**1335**	DKC335L	**1367**	DKC367L
1239	BKC239K	**1272**	BKC272K	**1304**	DKC304L	**1336**	DKC336L	**1368**	DKC368L
1240	BKC240K	**1273**	BKC273K	**1305**	DKC305L	**1337**	DKC337L	**1369**	DKC369L
1241	BKC241K	**1274**	BKC274K	**1306**	DKC306L	**1338**	DKC338L	**1370**	DKC370L
1242	BKC242K	**1275**	BKC275K	**1307**	DKC307L	**1339**	DKC339L	**1371**	DKC371L
1243	BKC243K	**1276**	BKC276K	**1308**	DKC308L	**1340**	DKC340L	**1372**	DKC372L
1244	BKC244K	**1277**	BKC277K	**1309**	DKC309L	**1341**	DKC341L	**1373**	DKC373L
1245	BKC245K	**1278**	BKC278K	**1310**	DKC310L	**1342**	DKC342L	**1374**	DKC374L
1246	BKC246K	**1279**	BKC279K	**1311**	DKC311L	**1343**	DKC343L	**1375**	DKC375L
1247	BKC247K	**1280**	BKC280K	**1312**	DKC312L	**1344**	DKC344L	**1376**	DKC376L
1248	BKC248K	**1281**	BKC281K	**1313**	DKC313L	**1345**	DKC345L	**1377**	DKC377L
1249	BKC249K	**1282**	BKC282K	**1314**	DKC314L	**1346**	DKC346L	**1378**	DKC378L
1250	BKC250K	**1283**	BKC283K	**1315**	DKC315L	**1347**	DKC347L	**1379**	DKC379L
1251	BKC251K	**1284**	BKC284K	**1316**	DKC316L	**1348**	DKC348L	**1380**	DKC380L
1252	BKC252K	**1285**	BKC285K	**1317**	DKC317L	**1349**	DKC349L	**1381**	DKC381L
1253	BKC253K	**1286**	BKC286K	**1318**	DKC318L	**1350**	DKC350L	**1382**	DKC382L
1254	BKC254K	**1287**	BKC287K	**1319**	DKC319L	**1352**	DKC352L	**1383**	DKC383L
1255	BKC255K	**1288**	BKC288K	**1320**	DKC320L	**1353**	DKC353L	**1384**	DKC384L
1256	BKC256K	**1289**	BKC289K	**1321**	DKC321L	**1354**	DKC354L	**1385**	DKC385L
1257	BKC257K	**1290**	BKC290K	**1322**	DKC322L	**1355**	DKC355L	**1386**	DKC386L
1258	BKC258K	**1291**	BKC291K	**1323**	DKC323L	**1356**	DKC356L	**1387**	DKC387L
1259	BKC259K	**1292**	BKC292K	**1324**	DKC324L	**1357**	DKC357L	**1388**	DKC388L
1260	BKC260K	**1293**	BKC293L	**1325**	DKC325L	**1358**	DKC358L	**1389**	DKC389L
1261	BKC261K	**1294**	BKC294K	**1326**b	DKC326L	**1359**	DKC359L	**1390**	DKC390L
1262	BKC262K	**1295**	BKC295K	**1327**	DKC327L	**1360**	DKC360L	**1391**	DKC391L
1263	BKC263K	**1296**	DKC296L	**1328**	DKC328L	**1361**	DKC361L	**1392**	DKC392L
1264	BKC264K	**1297**	DKC297L	**1329**	DKC329L	**1362**	DKC362L	**1393**	DKC393L
1265	BKC265K	**1298**	DKC298L	**1330**a	DKC330L	**1363**	DKC363L	**1394**	DKC394L
1267	BKC267K	**1299**	DKC299L	**1331**	DKC331L	**1364**	DKC364L	**1395**	DKC395L
1268	BKC268K	**1300**	DKC300L	**1332**	DKC332L				

a Advertisement for St Helens Glass   b Advertisement for Johnstone's Paints

1396–1445

Chassis Leyland Atlantean AN68/1R
Bodywork East Lancs H43/32F

Built 1973
Number in Stock 49

1396	EKD396L	**1406**	EKD406L	**1416**	EKD416L	**1426**	EKD426L	**1436**	EKD436L
1397	EKD397L	**1407**	EKD407L	**1417**	EKD417L	**1427**	EKD427L	**1437**	EKD437L
1398	EKD398L	**1408**	EKD408L	**1418**	EKD418L	**1428**	EKD428L	**1439**	EKD439L
1399	EKD399L	**1409**	EKD409L	**1419**	EKD419L	**1429**	EKD429L	**1440**	EKD440L
1400	EKD400L	**1410**	EKD410L	**1420**	EKD420L	**1430**	EKD430L	**1441**	EKD441L
1401	EKD401L	**1411**	EKD411L	**1421**	EKD421L	**1431**	EKD431L	**1442**	EKD442L
1402	EKD402L	**1412**	EKD412L	**1422**	EKD422L	**1432**	EKD432L	**1443**	EKD443L
1403	EKD403L	**1413**	EKD413L	**1423**	EKD423L	**1433**	EKD433L	**1444**	EKD444L
1404	EKD404L	**1414**	EKD414L	**1424**	EKD424L	**1434**	EKD434L	**1445**	EKD445L
1405	EKD405L	**1415**	EKD415L	**1425**	EKD425L	**1435**	EKD435L		

1446–1685

Chassis Leyland Atlantean AN68/1R
Bodywork Alexander H43/32F
(1551 is being converted to O43/32F)

Built 1973-6
Number in Stock 239

1446	GKA446L	**1494**	GKA494M	**1542**	GKA542M	**1590**	GKA15N	**1638**	HTJ638P
1447	GKA447L	**1495**	GKA495M	**1543**	GKA543M	**1591**	GKA16N	**1639**	HTJ639P
1448	GKA448L	**1496**	GKA496M	**1544**	GKA544M	**1592**	GKA17N	**1640**	HTJ640P
1449	GKA449L	**1497**	GKA497M	**1545**	GKA545M	**1593**	GKA18N	**1641**	HTJ641P
1450	GKA450L	**1498**	GKA498M	**1546**	OLV546M	**1594**	GKA19N	**1642**	HTJ642P
1451	GKA451L	**1499**	GKA499M	**1547**	OLV547M	**1595**	GKA20N	**1643**	HTJ643P
1452	GKA452L	**1500**	GKA500M	**1548**d	OLV548M	**1596**	GKA21N	**1644**	HTJ644P
1453	GKA453L	**1501**	GKA501M	**1549**	OLV549M	**1597**	GKA22N	**1645**	HTJ645P
1454	GKA454L	**1502**	GKA502M	**1550**	OLV550M	**1598**	GKA23N	**1646**	HTJ646P
1455	GKA455L	**1503**	GKA503M	**1551**	OLV551M	**1599**	GKA24N	**1647**	HTJ647P
1456	GKA456L	**1504**	GKA504M	**1552**	OLV552M	**1600**	GKA25N	**1648**	HTJ648P
1457	GKA457L	**1505**	GKA505M	**1553**	OLV553M	**1601**	GKA26N	**1649**	HTJ649P
1458	GKA458L	**1506**	GKA506M	**1554**	PKB554M	**1602**	GKA27N	**1650**	HTJ650P
1459	GKA459L	**1507**	GKA507M	**1555**	PKB555M	**1603**	GKA28N	**1651**	HTJ651P
1460	GKA460L	**1508**	GKA508M	**1556**	PKB556M	**1604**	GKA29N	**1652**	HTJ652P
1461	GKA461L	**1509**	GKA509M	**1557**	PKB557M	**1605**	GKA30N	**1653**	HTJ653P
1462	GKA462L	**1510**	GKA510M	**1558**	PKB558M	**1606**	GKA31N	**1654**	HTJ654P
1463	GKA463L	**1511**	GKA511M	**1559**	PKB559M	**1607**	GKA32N	**1655**	HTJ655P
1464	GKA464L	**1512**	GKA512M	**1560**	PKB560M	**1608**	GKA33N	**1656**	HTJ656P
1465	GKA465L	**1513**	GKA513M	**1561**	PKB561M	**1609**	GKA34N	**1657**	HTJ657P
1466	GKA466L	**1514**	GKA514M	**1562**	PKB562M	**1610**	GKA35N	**1658**	HTJ658P
1467	GKA467L	**1515**	GKA515M	**1563**	PKB563M	**1611**	GKA36N	**1659**	HTJ659P
1468	GKA468L	**1516**	GKA516M	**1564**	PKB564M	**1612**	GKA37N	**1660**	HTJ660P
1469	GKA469L	**1517**	GKA517M	**1565**	PKB565M	**1613**	GKA38N	**1661**	HTJ661P
1470	GKA470L	**1518**	GKA518M	**1566**	PKB566M	**1614**	GKA39N	**1662**	HTJ662P
1471	GKA471L	**1519**	GKA519M	**1567**	PKB567M	**1615**	GKA40N	**1663**	HTJ663P
1472	GKA472L	**1520**	GKA520M	**1568**	PKB568M	**1616**	GKA41N	**1664**	HTJ664P
1473	GKA473L	**1521**b	GKA521M	**1569**	PKB569M	**1617**	GKA42N	**1665**	HTJ665P
1474	GKA474L	**1522**	GKA522M	**1570**	PKB570N	**1618**	GKA43N	**1666**	HTJ666P
1475	GKA475L	**1523**	GKA523M	**1571**	RKA575N	**1619**	GKA44N	**1667**	HTJ667P
1476	GKA476L	**1524**	GKA524M	**1572**	RKA576N	**1620**	GKA45N	**1668**	HTJ668P
1477	GKA477L	**1525**	GKA525M	**1573**	RKA577N	**1621**	GKA46N	**1669**	HTJ669P
1478	GKA478L	**1526**	GKA526M	**1574**	RKA578N	**1622**	GKA47N	**1670**	HTJ670P
1479	GKA479L	**1527**	GKA527M	**1575**	RKA579N	**1623**	GKA48N	**1672**	HTJ672P
1480	GKA480L	**1528**	GKA528M	**1576**	RKA580N	**1624**	GKA49N	**1673**	HTJ673P
1481	GKA481M	**1529**	GKA529M	**1577**	RKA581N	**1625**	GKA50N	**1674**	HTJ674P
1482	GKA482L	**1530**	GKA530M	**1578**	RKA582N	**1626**	HTJ626P	**1675**	HTJ675P
1483	GKA483L	**1531**	GKA531M	**1579**	RKA583N	**1627**	HTJ627P	**1676**	HTJ676P
1484a	GKA484L	**1532**c	GKA532M	**1580**	RKA584N	**1628**	HTJ628P	**1677**	HTJ677P
1485	GKA485L	**1533**	GKA533M	**1581**	RKA585N	**1629**	HTJ629P	**1678**	HTJ678P
1486	GKA486M	**1534**	GKA534M	**1582**	RKA586N	**1630**	HTJ630P	**1679**	HTJ679P
1487	GKA487M	**1535**	GKA535M	**1583**	RKA587N	**1631**	HTJ631P	**1680**	HTJ680P
1488	GKA488M	**1536**	GKA536M	**1584**	RKA588N	**1632**	HTJ632P	**1681**	HTJ681P
1489	GKA489M	**1537**	GKA537M	**1585**	RKA589N	**1633**	HTJ633P	**1682**	HTJ682P
1490	GKA490M	**1538**	GKA538M	**1586**	GKA11N	**1634**	HTJ634P	**1683**	HTJ683P
1491	GKA491M	**1539**	GKA539M	**1587**	GKA12N	**1635**	HTJ635P	**1684**	HTJ684P
1492	GKA492M	**1540**	GKA540M	**1588**	GKA13N	**1636**	HTJ636P	**1685**	HTJ685P
1493	GKA493M	**1541**	GKA541M	**1589**	GKA14N	**1637**	HTJ637P		

a Advertisement for MPD Hampers
b Advertisement for Liverpool City Entertainments
c Advertisement for Fiesta Hampers
d Advertisement for Phoenix Assurance

1686–1842

Chassis Leyland Atlantean AN68/1R (1686-1725)
AN68A/1R (1726-1842)
Bodywork East Lancs H43/32F (1686-1765, 1840)
East Lancs H45/33F (1821-39/41/2)
Metro-Cammell Weymann H49/31F (1776)
H43/32F (1777-1820)

Built 1976-80
Number in Stock 147

1686	JWM686P	**1703**	JWM703P	**1720**	JWM720P	**1737**	LKF737R	**1754**	LKF754R
1687	JWM687P	**1704**	JWM704P	**1721**	JWM721P	**1738**	LKF738R	**1755**	LKF755R
1688	JWM688P	**1705**	JWM705P	**1722**	JWM722P	**1739**	LKF739R	**1756**	MTJ756S
1689	JWM689P	**1706**	JWM706P	**1723**	JWM723P	**1740**	LKF740R	**1757**	MTJ757S
1690	JWM690P	**1707**	JWM707P	**1724**	JWM724P	**1741**	LKF741R	**1758**	MTJ758S
1691	JWM691P	**1708**	JWM708P	**1725**	JWM725P	**1742**	LKF742R	**1759**	MTJ759S
1692	JWM692P	**1709**	JWM709P	**1726**	LKF726R	**1743**	LKF743R	**1760**	MTJ760S
1693	JWM693P	**1710**	JWM710P	**1727**	LKF727R	**1744**	LKF744R	**1761**	MTJ761S
1694	JWM694P	**1711**	JWM711P	**1728**	LKF728R	**1745**	LKF745R	**1762**	MTJ762S
1695	JWM695P	**1712**	JWM712P	**1729**	LKF729R	**1746**	LKF746R	**1763**	MTJ763S
1696	JWM696P	**1713**	JWM713P	**1730**	LKF730R	**1747**	LKF747R	**1764**	MTJ764S
1697	JWM697P	**1714**	JWM714P	**1731**	LKF731R	**1748**	LKF748R	**1765**	MTJ765S
1698	JWM698P	**1715**	JWM715P	**1732**	LKF732R	**1749**	LKF749R	**1776**	OEM776S
1699	JWM699P	**1716**	JWM716P	**1733**	LKF733R	**1750**	LKF750R	**1777**	OEM777S
1700	JWM700P	**1717**	JWM717P	**1734**	LKF734R	**1751**	LKF751R	**1778**	OEM778S
1701	JWM701P	**1718**	JWM718P	**1735**	LKF735R	**1752**	LKF752R	**1779**	OEM779S
1702	JWM702P	**1719**	JWM719P	**1736**	LKF736R	**1753**	LKF753R	**1780**	OEM780S

Listing continues

1781	OEM781S	**1794**	OEM794S	**1807**	PKA721S	**1820**	PHF561T	**1833**	TWM217V
1782	OEM782S	**1795**	OEM795S	**1808**	PKA722S	**1821**	RBG821T	**1834**	WWM917W
1783	OEM783S	**1796**	OEM796S	**1809**	PKA723S	**1822**	TWM209V	**1835**	TWM219V
1784a	OEM784S	**1797**	OEM797S	**1810**	PKA724S	**1823**	TWM210V	**1836**	TWM220V
1785	OEM785S	**1798**	OEM798S	**1811**	PKA725S	**1824**	TWM211V	**1837**	RBG837T
1786	OEM786S	**1799**	OEM799S	**1812**	PKA726S	**1825**	RBG825T	**1838**	RBG838T
1787	OEM787S	**1800**	OEM800S	**1813**	PKA727S	**1826**	RBG826T	**1839**	RBG839T
1788	OEM788S	**1801**	OEM801S	**1814**	PKA728S	**1827**	RBG827T	**1840**	RBG840T
1789b	OEM789S	**1802**	OEM802S	**1815**	PKA729S	**1828**	TWM212V	**1841**	RBG841T
1790	OEM790S	**1803**	OEM803S	**1816**	PHF557T	**1829**	TWM213V	**1842**	TWM221V
1791	OEM791S	**1804**	OEM804S	**1817**	PHF558T	**1830**	TWM214V		
1792	OEM792S	**1805**	OEM805S	**1818**	PHF559T	**1831**	TWM215V		
1793	OEM793S	**1806**	PKA720S	**1819**	PHF560T	**1832**	TWM216V		

a Advertisement for Broseley Estates b Wallasey Corporation livery

1843–1991

Chassis Leyland Atlantean AN68B/1R (1843-1967)
AN68D/1R (1968-91)
Bodywork Willowbrook H45/33F (1843-72)
Alexander H43/32F (1873-1991)

Built 1980-2
Number in Stock 149

1843	WWM920W	**1873**	XEM873W	**1903**	XEM903W	**1933**	ACM733X	**1963**	ACM763X
1844	WWM921W	**1874**	XEM874W	**1904**	XEM904W	**1934**	ACM734X	**1964**	ACM764X
1845	WWM922W	**1875**	XEM875W	**1905**	XEM905W	**1935**	ACM735X	**1965**	ACM765X
1846	WWM923W	**1876**	XEM876W	**1906**	XEM906W	**1936**	ACM736X	**1966**	ACM766X
1847	WWM924W	**1877**	XEM877W	**1907**	XEM907W	**1937**	ACM737X	**1967**	ACM767X
1848	WWM925W	**1878**	XEM878W	**1908**	XEM908W	**1938**	ACM738X	**1968**	DKF683X
1849	WWM926W	**1879**	XEM879W	**1909**	XEM909W	**1939**	ACM739X	**1969**	DKF684X
1850	WWM927W	**1880**	XEM880W	**1910**	XEM910W	**1940**	ACM740X	**1970**	DKF685X
1851	WWM928W	**1881**	XEM881W	**1911**	XEM911W	**1941**	ACM741X	**1971**	EKA171Y
1852	WWM929W	**1882**	XEM882W	**1912**	XEM912W	**1942**	ACM742X	**1972**	EKA172Y
1853	WWM930W	**1883**	XEM883W	**1913**	ACM713X	**1943**	ACM743X	**1973**	DEM773Y
1854	WWM931W	**1884**	XEM884W	**1914**	ACM714X	**1944**	ACM744X	**1974**	DEM774Y
1855	WWM932W	**1885**	XEM885W	**1915**	ACM715X	**1945**	ACM745X	**1975**	DEM775Y
1856	WWM933W	**1886**	XEM886W	**1916**	ACM716X	**1946**	ACM746X	**1976**	DEM776Y
1857	WWM934W	**1887**	XEM887W	**1917**	ACM717X	**1947**	ACM747X	**1977**	DEM777Y
1858	WWM935W	**1888**	XEM888W	**1918**	ACM718X	**1948**	ACM748X	**1978**	DEM778Y
1859	WWM936W	**1889**	XEM889W	**1919**	ACM719X	**1949**	ACM749X	**1979**	DEM779Y
1860	AFY180X	**1890**	XEM890W	**1920**	ACM720X	**1950**	ACM750X	**1980**	DEM780Y
1861	AFY181X	**1891**	XEM891W	**1921**	ACM721X	**1951**	ACM751X	**1981**	DEM781Y
1862	AFY182X	**1892**	XEM892W	**1922**	ACM722X	**1952**	ACM752X	**1982**	DEM782Y
1863	AFY183X	**1893**	XEM893W	**1923**	ACM723X	**1953**	ACM753X	**1983**	DEM783Y
1864	AFY184X	**1894**	XEM894W	**1924**	ACM724X	**1954**	ACM754X	**1984**	DEM784Y
1865	AFY185X	**1895**	XEM895W	**1925**	ACM725X	**1955**	ACM755X	**1985**	DEM785Y
1866	AFY186X	**1896**	XEM896W	**1926**	ACM726X	**1956**	ACM756X	**1986**	DEM786Y
1867	AFY187X	**1897**	XEM897W	**1927**	ACM727X	**1957**	ACM757X	**1987**	DEM787Y
1868	AFY188X	**1898**	XEM898W	**1928**	ACM728X	**1958**	ACM758X	**1988**	DEM788Y
1869	AFY189X	**1899**	XEM899W	**1929**	ACM729X	**1959**	ACM759X	**1989**	DEM789Y
1870	AFY190X	**1900**	XEM900W	**1930**	ACM730X	**1960**	ACM760X	**1990**	DEM790Y
1871	AFY191X	**1901**	XEM901W	**1931**	ACM731X	**1961**	ACM761X	**1991**	DEM791Y
1872	AFY192X	**1902**	XEM902W	**1932**	ACM732X	**1962**	ACM762X		

2026–2080

Chassis Bristol VRT/LH2/6LX
Bodywork East Lancs H49/31D

Built 1970/1
Number in Stock 4

2026	UKD520J	**2028**	UKD522H	**2043**	UKD537J	**2080**	YKF718K

2086–2094

Chassis Bristol RESL6L
Bodywork Eastern Coachworks B44F

Built 1971
Number in Stock 3

2086	YKB361J	**2093**	YKB368J	**2094**	YKB369J

2096–2145

Chassis Bristol VRT/SL2/6LX
Bodywork East Lancs H43/32F

Built 1974/5
Number in Stock 50

2096	RKB96N	**2106**	GKA58N	**2116**	GKA68N	**2126**	GKA78N	**2136**	GKA88N
2097	RKB97N	**2107**	GKA59N	**2117**	GKA69N	**2127**	GKA79N	**2137**	GKA89N
2098	RKB98N	**2108**	GKA60N	**2118**	GKA70N	**2128**	GKA80N	**2138**	GKA90N
2099	GKA51N	**2109**	GKA61N	**2119**	GKA71N	**2129**	GKA81N	**2139**	GKA91N
2100	GKA52N	**2110**	GKA62N	**2120**	GKA72N	**2130**	GKA82N	**2140**	GKA92N
2101	GKA53N	**2111**	GKA63N	**2121**	GKA73N	**2131**	GKA83N	**2141**	GKA93N
2102	GKA54N	**2112**	GKA64N	**2122**	GKA74N	**2132**	GKA84N	**2142**	GKA94N
2103	GKA55N	**2113**	GKA65N	**2123**	GKA75N	**2133**	GKA85N	**2143**	GKA95N
2104	GKA56N	**2114**	GKA66N	**2124**	GKA76N	**2134**	GKA86N	**2144**	GKA96N
2105	GKA57N	**2115**	GKA67N	**2125**	GKA77N	**2135**	GKA87N	**2145**	GKA97N

2146–2155

Chassis Bristol RESL6G
Bodywork Eastern Coachworks B47F

Built 1975
Number in Stock 10

2146	GTJ382N	**2148**	GTJ384N	**2150**	GTJ386N	**2152**	GTJ388N	**2154**	GTJ390N
2147	GTJ383N	**2149**	GTJ385N	**2151**	GTJ387N	**2153**	GTJ389N	**2155**	GTJ391N

2156–2160

Chassis Bristol LHS6L
Bodywork Eastern Coachworks B27F
Acquired from West Yorkshire PTE (36/8, 44/5) in 1980

Built 1975/6
Number in Stock 4

2156	JUG352N	**2158**	JUG354N	**2159**	MUA44P	**2160**	MUA45P

3001–3050

Chassis Daimler Fleetline CRG6LXB
Bodywork Metro-Cammell Weymann H43/32F
3011-20 (CKC311-20L) are on permanent loan to Crosville

Built 1973
Number in Stock 40

3001	CKC301L	**3009**	CKC309L	**3027**	CKC327L	**3035**	CKC335L	**3043**	CKC343L
3002	CKC302L	**3010**	CKC310L	**3028**	CKC328L	**3036**	CKC336L	**3044**	CKC344L
3003	CKC303L	**3021**	CKC321L	**3029**	CKC329L	**3037**	CKC337L	**3045**	CKC345L
3004	CKC304L	**3022**	CKC322L	**3030**	CKC330L	**3038**	CKC338L	**3046**	CKC346L
3005t	CKC305L	**3023**	CKC323L	**3031**	CKC331L	**3039**	CKC339L	**3047**	CKC347L
3006	CKC306L	**3024**	CKC324L	**3032**	CKC332L	**3040**	CKC340L	**3048**	CKC348L
3007	CKC307L	**3025**	CKC325L	**3033**	CKC333L	**3041**	CKC341L	**3049**	CKC349L
3008	CKC308L	**3026**	CKC326L	**3034**	CKC334L	**3042**	CKC342L	**3050**	CKC350L

t Training bus

4001–4020

Chassis Metro Scania BR111MH
Bodywork Metro-Cammell Weymann B47F (4001-8)
B44F (4009-20)

Built 1972
Number in Stock 15

4001	CKD401L	**4006**	CKD406L	**4011**	CKD411L	**4015**	CKD415L	**4018**	CKD418L
4002	CKD402L	**4008**	CKD408L	**4012**	CKD412L	**4016**	CKD416L	**4019**	CKD419L
4003	CKD403L	**4010**	CKD410L	**4013**	CKD413L	**4017**	CKD417L	**4020**	CKD420L

4021–4080

Chassis Metropolitan BR111DH
Bodywork Metro-Cammell Weymann H44/29F

Built 1974/5
Number in Stock 44

4021	OKD579M	**4040**	RKA440N	**4052**	HWM52P	**4063**	HWM63P	**4073**	HWM73P
4022	PKD422M	**4042**	HBG481N	**4053**	HWM53P	**4064**	HWM64P	**4074**	HWM74P
4023	PKD423M	**4043**	HBG482N	**4054**	HWM54P	**4065**	HWM65P	**4075**	HWM75P
4025	PKD425M	**4044**	HBG483N	**4055**	HWM55P	**4067**	HWM67P	**4076**	HWM76P
4026	PKD426M	**4045**	HWM45P	**4056**	HWM56P	**4068**	HWM68P	**4077**	HWM77P
4030	PKD430M	**4046**	HWM46P	**4057**	HWM57P	**4069**	HWM69P	**4078**	HWM78P
4035	RKA435N	**4047**	HWM47P	**4058**	HWM58P	**4070**	HWM70P	**4079**	HWM79P
4038	RKA438N	**4049**	HWM49P	**4061**	HWM61P	**4071**	HWM71P	**4080**	HWM80P
4039	RKA439N	**4050**	HWM50P	**4062**	HWM62P	**4072**	HWM72P		

6001–6034

Chassis Leyland National 11351A/1R
Bodywork Leyland National B49F

Built 1979
Number in Stock 34

6001	SKF1T	**6008**	SKF8T	**6015**	SKF15T	**6022**	SKF22T	**6029**	SKF29T
6002	SKF2T	**6009**	SKF9T	**6016**	SKF16T	**6023**	SKF23T	**6030**	SKF30T
6003	SKF3T	**6010**	SKF10T	**6017**	SKF17T	**6024**	SKF24T	**6031**	SKF31T
6004	SKF4T	**6011**	SKF11T	**6018**	SKF18T	**6025**	SKF25T	**6032**	SKF32T
6005	SKF5T	**6012**	SKF12T	**6019**	SKF19T	**6026**	SKF26T	**6033**	SKF33T
6006	SKF6T	**6013**	SKF13T	**6020**	SKF20T	**6027**	SKF27T	**6034**	SKF34T
6007	SKF7T	**6014**	SKF14T	**6021**	SKF21T	**6028**	SKF28T		

6035–6041

Chassis Leyland National 2 NL116L11/1R
Bodywork Leyland National B49F

Built 1979/80
Number in Stock 7

6035	UEM35V	**6037**	UEM37V	**6039**	UEM39V	**6040**	UEM40V	**6041**	UEM41V
6036	UEM36V	**6038**	UEM38V						

6042–6049

Chassis Leyland National 1151/2R
Bodywork Leyland National B49F
Acquired from Southport Corporation (1-8) in 1974 as B46D
Built 1974
Number in Stock 8

6042	YFY1M	**6044**	YFY3M	**6046**	YFY5M	**6048**	YFM7M	**6049**	YFM8M
6043	YFY2M	**6045**	YFY4M	**6047**	YFY6M				

6050–6079

Chassis Leyland National 11351A/1R
Bodywork Leyland National B49F
Built 1977/8
Number in Stock 30

6050	MTJ766S	**6056**	MTJ772S	**6062**	RKA868T	**6068**	RKA874T	**6074**	RKA880T
6051	MTJ767S	**6057**	MTJ773S	**6063**	RKA869T	**6069**	RKA875T	**6075**	RKA881T
6052	MTJ768S	**6058**	MTJ774S	**6064**	RKA870T	**6070**	RKA876T	**6076**	RKA882T
6053	MTJ769S	**6059**	MTJ775S	**6065**	RKA871T	**6071**	RKA877T	**6077**	RKA883T
6054	MTJ770S	**6060**	RKA866T	**6066**	RKA872T	**6072**	RKA878T	**6078**	RKA884T
6055a	MTJ771S	**6061**	RKA867T	**6067**	RKA873T	**6073**	RKA879T	**6079**	RKA885T

a Advertisement for St Helens Glass

6080–6173

Chassis Leyland National 2 NL116AL11/1R
Bodywork Leyland National B49F
Built 1980-2
Number in Stock 94

6080	VBG80V	**6099**	VBG99V	**6118**	VBG118V	**6137**	WWM915W	**6156**	XLV156W
6081	VBG81V	**6100**	WWM905W	**6119**	VBG119V	**6138**	WWM916W	**6157**	XLV157W
6082	VBG82V	**6101**	VBG101V	**6120**	VBG120V	**6139**	XLV139W	**6158**	XLV158W
6083	VBG83V	**6102**	VBG102V	**6121**	VBG121V	**6140**	XLV140W	**6159**	XLV159W
6084	VBG84V	**6103**	VBG103V	**6122**	VBG122V	**6141**	XLV141W	**6160**	XLV160W
6085	VBG85V	**6104**	VBG104V	**6123**	WWM906W	**6142**	XLV142W	**6161**	XLV161W
6086	VBG86V	**6105**	VBG105V	**6124**	WWM907W	**6143**	XLV143W	**6162**	XLV162W
6087	VBG87V	**6106**	VBG106V	**6125**	WWM908W	**6144**	XLV144W	**6163**	XLV163W
6088	VBG88V	**6107**	VBG107V	**6126**	WWM909W	**6145**	XLV145W	**6164**	CKB161X
6089	VBG89V	**6108**	VBG108V	**6127**	VBG127V	**6146**	XLV146W	**6165**	CKB162X
6090	VBG90V	**6109**	VBG109V	**6128**	VBG128V	**6147**	XLV147W	**6166**	CKB163X
6091	VBG91V	**6110**	VBG110V	**6129**	VBG129V	**6148**	XLV148W	**6167**	CKB164X
6092	VBG92V	**6111**	VBG111V	**6130**	VBG130V	**6149**	XLV149W	**6168**	CKB165X
6093	VBG93V	**6112**	VBG112V	**6131**	WWM910W	**6150**	XLV150W	**6169**	CKB166X
6094	VBG94V	**6113**	VBG113V	**6132**	WWM911W	**6151**	XLV151W	**6170**	CKB167X
6095	VBG95V	**6114**	VBG114V	**6133**	VBG133V	**6152**	XLV152W	**6171**	CKB168X
6096	VBG96V	**6115**	VBG115V	**6134**	WWM912W	**6153**	XLV153W	**6172**	CKB169X
6097	VBG97V	**6116**	VBG116V	**6135**	WWM913W	**6154**	XLV154W	**6173**	CKB170X
6098	VBG98V	**6117**	VBG117V	**6136**	WWM914W	**6155**	XLV155W		

7000–7002

Chassis Leyland National 11351A/1R
Bodywork Leyland National DP45F
Built 1978
Number in Stock 3

7000	OHF858S	**7001**	RKA886T	**7002**	RKA887T

7003

Chassis Leyland Leopard PSU3E/4R
Bodywork Duple C49F
Built 1980
Number in Stock 1

7003	WWM576W

7004–7007

Chassis Leyland National 2 NL116AL11/1R
Bodywork Leyland National DP44F
Built 1981
Number in Stock 4

7004	XTJ4W	**7005**	XTJ5W	**7006**	XTJ6W	**7007**	XTJ7W

7008

Chassis Leyland Leopard PSU3E/4R
Bodywork Duple C49F
Built 1981
Number in Stock 1

7008	YKA8W

7009–7020

Chassis Leyland Tiger TRCTL11/2R
Bodywork Duple C49F
Built 1982
Number in Stock 12

7009	CKC623X	**7012**	CKC626X	**7015**	EKA215Y	**7017**	EKA217Y	**7019**	EKA219Y
7010	CKC625X	**7013**	CKC624X	**7016**	EKA216Y	**7018**	EKA218Y	**7020**	EKA220Y
7011	CKC627X	**7014**	CKC628X						

NATIONAL TRAVEL WEST

National Travel (West) Ltd operates express services from the western side of the country stretching from the Lake District in the north down through Lancashire, Merseyside, Greater Manchester, the western Midlands to Cheltenham and Bristol. Its history is as complex as its operating area suggests. Predecessors which have contributed range from erstwhile well-known BET companies such as North Western, Standerwick and Black & White to independents like Scout, Don Everall and Worthington Motor Tours. On the way, services and vehicles have also been acquired from former Tilling companies, in particular Bristol and Crosville.

National Travel (West) can be directly traced back in financial terms to the Macclesfield branch of the British Automobile Traction Company which commenced operations on 10th November 1913, to become the North Western Road Car Company Ltd on 23rd April 1923. Through a series of renamings this company is today National Travel (West). Although principally a bus operator to the south and east of Manchester and the Peak District, a network of express routes from the area was developed by North Western. However, it was not until 1933 that the principal Manchester-Birmingham-London service was jointly acquired with Midland Red from Majestic Motors, and even then the latter remained in existence as a separate jointly-owned subsidiary until 1953. In early 1972 North Western's bus services were transferred to Crosville, SELNEC PTE and Trent, thus leaving it purely as an express operator from 4th March 1972. The company was renamed National Travel (North West) on 6th February 1974 and acquired the vehicles of W.C. Standerwick Ltd, Preston.

Standerwick started operations from Blackpool in 1908 and was very early in the field of long-distance tours. In 1932 control was gained by Ribble Motor Services together with several other Blackpool operators which were merged with Standerwick. This continued to operate as a separate company, mainly concentrating on express services from Blackpool and the Lake District to London and Birmingham. Scout Motor Services of Preston, which remained independent until Ribble took control in 1961, had operated both bus and coach services in the Preston and Blackpool areas, which from the early 1940s onwards were jointly operated with Ribble (buses) and Standerwick (coaches). In October 1968 the express vehicles were acquired by Standerwick and the buses by Ribble. Standerwick were noted in the 1960s and 1970s for the operation of double deck coaches on the London motorway services, the first generation being Leyland Atlantean/Weymann "Gay Hostesses" replaced later by the unique Bristol VRL/ECW vehicles.

National Travel (North West) was again renamed National Travel (West) on 1st April 1977 to reflect the acquisition of National Travel (Midlands) based in Birmingham. This company had been activated as recently as December 1973, being the South Midland Motor Services renamed.

Initially it had no vehicles, but in January 1974 purchased Worthington Motor Tours Ltd of Birmingham and Don Everall Travel Ltd of Wolverhampton. Both firms concentrated on excursions and tours and had early origins, Everall going back to 1919 (commencing with taxis) and Worthington to 1923, becoming limited companies in 1934 and 1938 respectively.

In both cases the major expansion of the excursions and tours business was in the post-war years, but Everall achieved this by purchasing many small operators scattered over the Black Country, whereas Worthington expanded its own programme and fleet.

National Travel (West) took over the operation of the Liverpool to London and Birmingham services of Crosville and Ribble in March 1980 and acquired some vehicles from both operators.

August 1981 saw National Travel (West) make its biggest expansion yet with the takeover of National Travel (South West) operations from Cheltenham and Bristol. The history of this company is as complex as that of National Travel (West) since it had expanded to cover operations in much of the West Country (Exeter, Torbay and Plymouth), Swansea, Bournemouth and Southampton as well as Cheltenham and Bristol. However, in May 1981 the West Country operations were handed over to Western National, South Wales to South Wales Transport and Bournemouth/Southampton to Hants and Dorset, and therefore the history and development of these sections are not part of this story.

National Travel (South West) was formed in February 1974 by the renaming of Black and White Motorways Ltd which had operated services on behalf of Associated Motorways from Cheltenham since July 1934, when the new coach station was opened in that town. Black and White started in 1928 and expanded its express services greatly until in April 1930 it was acquired by Midland Red. Shortly afterwards Bristol Tramways and City of Oxford took shares in the company. Black and White was well known in the 1930s and 1940s for its interesting use of Bristol L6Gs with Duple bodywork, an unusual combination for use on express services.

A new company, Wessex National, was formed in August 1974 by the renaming of the erstwhile Bath Tramways Motor Company and it then acquired the business of Wessex Coaches Limited, Bristol which had been formed in August 1947 by the amalgamation of four local excursions and tours businesses. Two of the companies had been operating charabancs as long ago as 1919. Management control of Wessex National was exercised by National Travel (South West) from its inception but all the vehicles were acquired by the parent company in March 1978.

In September 1978 National Travel (South West) acquired the express services and vehicles based on Bristol from Bristol Omnibus. Most of these services had originated from Greyhound Motors of Bristol which had been controlled by Bristol Tramways from 1928 and was fully absorbed by the parent company in January 1936. The Greyhound fleetname continued in use until the 1970s however.

When National Travel (South West) was taken over by National Travel (West) it was decided that Cheltenham based vehicles would use the fleetname Black and White and that those based on Bristol would use the fleetname Wessex. Accordingly, vehicles are receiving these names on repainting.

The Leyland Leopard with Duple, Plaxton and Willowbrook coachwork has been the mainstay of the National Travel (West) fleet, including a high proportion of 12-metre long coaches. An interesting reversion to Standerwick practice has been the purchase of a Leyland Olympian/ECW double deck coach which is currently being evaluated on the Bristol-London service. Other interesting coaches undergoing evaluation are Dennis Falcon Vs.

Fleet livery is standard National Express white. Some vehicles are in National Holidays livery, while those employed on Manchester-London Rapide services also are in a distinctive livery. Depots are situated at Blackpool, Bristol, Cheltenham, Liverpool and Manchester.

National Travel West No. 79 is one of sixteen Leyland Leopard PSU5s with Plaxton coachwork delivered in 1980/1. Fleet renumbering took place early in 1983 and No. 79 was originally numbered N279, which it carries in this photograph taken in Lancaster. P.R. Gainsbury

In 1981 ten Duple Dominant/Leyland Leopard PSU5s were purchased and N282 (now 82) is seen at Victoria coach station, London on the Rapide service from Manchester. The fitting on the roof towards the front houses video equipment. D. Savage

Further variety in bodywork on the Leyland Leopard PSU5 chassis is provided by the Eastern Coachworks design seen on No. 91. This vehicle was photographed at Wembley. G.R. Mills

Now numbered 95, National Travel West's first Leyland Tiger was originally numbered N60. It was built in 1982 and has Duple Dominant bodywork with two video units. It is seen in Liverpool. R.L. Wilson

Two Dennis Falcons have recently been placed in service by National Travel West, both with Duple Goldliner bodies. They are numbered 99 and 100 in the fleet and the first of the pair is seen at London Victoria. B.J. Hemming

No. 156 is one of a number of National Travel West coaches to carry the distinctive Willowbrook Spacecar body on a Leyland Leopard chassis. It is seen in Lancaster. P.R. Gainsbury

Several Duple Dominant bodied Leyland Leopard PSU3s were acquired from Crosville and Ribble in 1980 when National Travel West took over direct responsibility for the express services radiating from Liverpool. No. 174 of 1976 was one of the latter and is seen here in a promotional white, red and blue Merseyside to North Wales livery. It was formerly Ribble 1074. R.L. Wilson

The new Leyland Tigers (200-205) carry similar bodywork to the most recent batch of Leopards. No. 203 displays the latest 'stripes' livery and the Black & White fleetname. D. Savage

The Plaxton bodied Leyland Leopard PSU3 is represented by No. 231 seen at Bournemouth in June 1983. This was among the coaches acquired from National Travel (South West) in 1981 and also now carries the Black & White fleetname. G.R. Mills

No. 403 is a Duple bodied Leopard PSU3, also taken over from the South West division of National Travel when it was merged with the West division in 1981. No. 403 is seen in Dorchester. G.R. Mills

Leaving Victoria coach station on the service from London to Plymouth is the Olympian coach No. 450. The striking bodywork is by Eastern Coachworks. D. Savage

NATIONAL TRAVEL (WEST) FLEET LIST

1–7

Chassis Leyland Leopard PSU5A/4R
Bodywork Plaxton C51F (6, 7: C48FT)
Built 1976
Number in Stock 7

1	SFV201P	**3**	SFV203P	**5**	SFV205P	**6**	SFV206P	**7**	SFV207P
2	SFV202P	**4**	SFV204P						

8–18

Chassis Leyland Leopard PSU5A/4R
Bodywork Duple C51F
Built 1976
Number in Stock 11

8	URN208R	**11**	URN211R	**13**	URN213R	**15**	URN215R	**17**	URN217R
9	URN209R	**12**	URN212R	**14**	URN214R	**16**	URN216R	**18**	URN218R
10	URN210R								

19–26

Chassis Leyland Leopard PSU5B/4R
Bodywork Willowbrook C51F
Built 1977
Number in Stock 8

19	XCK219R	**21**	XCK221R	**23**	SEA312R	**25**	WUE612S	**26**	WUE613S
20	XCK220R	**22**	SEA311R	**24**	WUE611S				

27–64

Chassis Leyland Leopard PSU5C/4R
Bodywork Duple C53F
(27/8: C45FT, 29-33: C51F, 34-48: C50F)

Built 1978-80
Number in Stock 38

27	VVU227S	**35**h	BNB235T	**43**h	BNB243T	**51**	HNE251V	**58**	JND258V
28	VVU228S	**36**	BNB236T	**44**	BNB244T	**52**	HNE252V	**59**	JND259V
29	VVU229S	**37**	BNB237T	**45**	BNB245T	**53**	HNE253V	**60**	JND260V
30	VVU230S	**38**	BNB238T	**46**h	BNB246T	**54**	HNE254V	**61**	JND261V
31	VVU231S	**39**	BNB239T	**47**h	BNB247T	**55**	HNE255V	**62**	JND262V
32	VVU232S	**40**	BNB240T	**48**h	BNB248T	**56**	JND256V	**63**h	JND263V
33	VVU233S	**41**	BNB241T	**49**	HNE249V	**57**h	JND257V	**64**	JND264V
34h	BNB234T	**42**h	BNB242T	**50**	HNE250V				

h National Holidays livery

65–80

Chassis Leyland Leopard PSU5D/4R
Bodywork Plaxton C53F (68-74: C50F)

Built 1980/1
Number in Stock 16

65h	MRJ265W	**69**h	MRJ269W	**72**h	MRJ272W	**75**h	MRJ275W	**78**	MRJ278W
66h	MRJ266W	**70**h	MRJ270W	**73**h	MRJ273W	**76**h	MRJ276W	**79**	MRJ279W
67h	MRJ267W	**71**h	MRJ271W	**74**h	MRJ274W	**77**	MRJ277W	**80**h	MRJ280W
68h	MRJ268W								

h National Holidays livery

81–90

Chassis Leyland Leopard PSU5D/4R
Bodywork Duple C50F

Built 1981
Number in Stock 10

81	SND281X	**83**	SND283X	**85**	SND285X	**87**	SND287X	**89**	SND289X
82	SND282X	**84**	SND284X	**86**	SND286X	**88**	SND288X	**90**h	SND290X

h National Holidays livery

91–94

Chassis Leyland Leopard PSU5E/4R
Bodywork Eastern Coachworks C53F

Built 1982/3
Number in Stock 4

91	ANA91Y	**92**	ANA92Y	**93**	ANA93Y	**94**	ANA94Y

95

Chassis Leyland Tiger TRCTL11/3R
Bodywork Duple C53F

Built 1982
Number in Stock 1

95	WVR60X

99/100

Chassis Dennis Falcon V SDA404
Bodywork Duple C47FT

Built 1982/3
Number in Stock 2

99	ANA99Y	**100**	ANA100Y

117–140

Chassis Leyland Leopard PSU3B/4R
Bodywork Duple C49F

Built 1974
Number in Stock 22

117	TTF217M	**124**	TTF224M	**129**	TTF229M	**133**	TTF233M	**137**	TTF237M
119w	TTF219M	**125**w	TTF225M	**130**	TTF230M	**134**	TTF234M	**138**	TTF238M
120	TTF220M	**126**	TTF226M	**131**	TTF231M	**135**w	TTF235M	**139**	TTF239M
122	TTF222M	**127**	TTF227M	**132**	TTF232M	**136**	TTF236M	**140**	TTF240M
123w	TTF223M	**128**	TTF228M						

141/142

Chassis Leyland Leopard PSU3B/4R
Bodywork Duple C49F
Ex-Ribble 1041/2 in 1977

Built 1974
Number in Stock 2

141	UTF721M	**142**	UTF722M

145–149

Chassis Leyland Leopard PSU3C/4R
Bodywork Duple C47F

Built 1976
Number in Stock 5

145	PCK145P	**146**	PCK146P	**147**	PCK147P	**148**	PCK148P	**149**	PCK149P

150–160

Chassis Leyland Leopard PSU3E/4R (150-2/8: PSU3D/4R)
Bodywork Willowbrook C47F (159/60: C28F)
158 ex-National Travel (Midlands) 1977

Built 1977
Number in Stock 11

150	XCW150R	**153**	XCW153R	**155**	XCW155R	**157**	XCW157R	**159**	VDH243S
151	XCW151R	**154**	XCW154R	**156**	XCW156R	**158**	PWD841R	**160**	VDH244S
152	XCW152R								

161–165

Chassis Leyland Leopard PSU3E/4R
Bodywork Duple C49F
Ex-Crosville CLL321-5 in 1980

Built 1977
Number in Stock 5

161	YTU321S	**162**	YTU322S	**163**	YTU323S	**164**	YTU324S	**165**	YTU325S

172–176

Chassis Leyland Leopard PSU3C/4R
Bodywork Duple C47F
Ex-Ribble 1072-6 in 1980

Built 1976
Number in Stock 5

172	PCW672P	**173**	PCW673P	**174**m	PCW674P	**175**	PCW675P	**176**	PCW676P

177–188

Chassis Leyland Leopard PSU3B/4R
Bodywork Duple C49F
177-9/82/3/6 ex-Standerwick 34-6/9, 40, 32 in 1974
184/7/8 ex-North Western 270/3/4 in 1974

Built 1973
Number in Stock 9

177w	XTF817L	**179**w	XTF819L	**183**	XTF823L	**186**w	XTF816L	**188**	XTF828L
178	XTF818L	**182**	XTF822L	**184**w	XTF824L	**187**	XTF827L		

190

Chassis Leyland Leopard PSU5/4R
Bodywork Alexander C44FT
Ex-Ribble 1200 in 1976

Built 1972
Number in Stock 1

190w	RTF561L

191/192

Chassis Leyland Leopard PSU3B/4R
Bodywork Duple C49F
Ex-Ribble 1025/6 in 1980

Built 1973
Number in Stock 2

191	WTF571L	**192**	WTF572L

193–197

Chassis Bristol RELH6L
Bodywork Eastern Coachworks C49F
Ex-North Western 13-17 in 1974

Built 1972
Number in Stock 5

193w	JMA413L	**194**w	JMA414L	**195**w	JMA415L	**196**w	JMA416L	**197**w	JMA417L

200–205

Chassis Leyland Tiger TRCTL11/3R
Bodywork Eastern Coachworks C53F

Built 1982/3
Number in Stock 6

200a	BDF200Y	**202**a	BDF202Y	**203**b	BDF203Y	**204**b	BDF204Y	**205**b	BDF205Y
201a	BDF201Y								

a Wessex fleetname b Black & White fleetname m Merseyside and North Wales livery

206/208

Chassis Leyland Tiger TRCTL11/3R
Bodywork Plaxton C50F

Built 1983
Number in Stock 2

206ah	CDG206Y	**208**ah	CDG208Y

220–226

Chassis Leyland Leopard PSU3B/4R
Bodywork Plaxton C47F
Ex-National Travel (South West) 220/3-6 in 1981

Built 1971
Number in Stock 5

220b YDF320K | **223**b YDF323K | **224**b YDF324K | **225**b YDF325K | **226**b YDF326K

230/231

Chassis Leyland Leopard PSU3A/4RT
Bodywork Plaxton C49F
Ex-National Travel (South West) 230/1 in 1981

Built 1970
Number in Stock 2

230b YTX322H | **231**b YTX323H

237–246

Chassis Leyland Leopard PSU3B/4R
Bodywork Plaxton C47F
Ex-National Travel (South West) same numbers in 1981

Built 1973
Number in Stock 7

237a FDF337L | **239**b FDF339L | **244**a FDF344L | **245**a FDF345L | **246**a FDF346L
238a FDF338L | **240**b FDF340L

248

Chassis Leyland Leopard PSU4B/4R
Bodywork Plaxton C40F
Ex-National Travel (South West) 248 in 1981

Built 1973
Number in Stock 1

248a HHA180L

253–276

Chassis Leyland Leopard PSU5C/4R
Bodywork Plaxton C57F
Ex-National Travel (South West) same numbers in 1981

Built 1979
Number in Stock 15

253ah DAD253T | **259**a DDG259T | **263**a FDF263T | **270**a EDF270T | **274**a EDF274T
256a DAD256T | **260**b DDG260T | **264**a FDF264T | **272**b EDF272T | **275**ah EDF275T
257a DAD257T | **262**a FDF262T | **267**a DDG267T | **273**ah EDF273T | **276**b EDF276T

277–286

Chassis Leyland Leopard PSU5C/4R
Bodywork Duple C50F
Ex-National Travel (South West) same numbers in 1981

Built 1979/80
Number in Stock 4

277b GDF277V | **279**ah GDF279V | **282**ah JDG282V | **286**b JDG286V

291–303

Chassis Leyland Leopard PSU5D/4R (291-4: PSU5C/4R)
Bodywork Plaxton C53F (291: C45F)

Built 1981
Number in Stock 13

291ah SND291X | **294**ah SND294X | **297**bh SND297X | **300**b SND300X | **302**b SND302X
292ah SND292X | **295**ah SND295X | **298**bp SND298X | **301**a SND301X | **303**b SND303X
293bh SND293X | **296**bp SND296X | **299**b SND299X

a Wessex fleetname | b Black & White fleetname | h National Holidays livery | p P & O livery

331–336

Chassis Leyland Leopard PSU3B/4R
Bodywork Plaxton C47F
Ex-National Travel (South West) same numbers in 1981

Built 1973/4
Number in Stock 3

331b LHU663L | **333**a RHY762M | **336**b RHY771M

345–359

Chassis Leyland Leopard PSU5C/4R
Bodywork Plaxton C57F
Ex-National Travel (South West) same numbers in 1981

Built 1980
Number in Stock 9

345a KAD345V | **348**b KAD348V | **353**b KAD353V | **357**a KAD357V | **359**b KAD359V
346b KAD346V | **352**a KAD352V | **355**b KAD355V | **358**b KAD358V

a Wessex fleetname | b Black & White fleetname

364–369

Chassis Leyland Leopard PSU3B/4R
Bodywork Plaxton C47F
Ex-National Travel (South West) 94, 95, 97-9 in 1981

Built 1974
Number in Stock 5

364a RHY764M	**365**a RHY765M	**367**a RHY767M	**368**a RHY768M	**369**a RHY769M

400–411

Chassis Leyland Leopard PSU3B/4R
Bodywork Duple C47F
Ex-National Travel (South West) 100-11 in 1981

Built 1974
Number in Stock 10

400b PDD100M	**402**b PDD102M	**404**b PDD404M	**406**b PDD406M	**410**a PDD410M
401b PDD101M	**403**b PDD103M	**405**b PDD405M	**409**a PDD409M	**411**b PDD411M

a Wessex fleetname   b Black & White fleetname

418–420

Chassis Leyland Leopard PSU3C/4R
Bodywork Duple C47F
Ex-National Travel (South West) 118-20 in 1981

Built 1976
Number in Stock 3

418b MDF118P	**419**ah MDF119P	**420**bh MDF120P

424–430

Chassis Leyland Leopard PSU3D/4R
Bodywork Willowbrook C47F
Ex-National Travel (South West) 124-30 in 1981

Built 1977
Number in Stock 7

424a SAD124R	**426**b SAD126R	**428**b SAD128R	**429**b SAD129R	**430**b SAD130R
425b SAD125R	**427**b SAD127R			

450

Chassis Leyland (Bristol) Olympian ONTL11/1R
Bodywork Eastern Coachworks CH45/20FT

Built 1982
Number in Stock 1

450a ADD50Y

455

Chassis AEC Reliance 6U2R
Bodywork Duple C57F
Ex-National Travel (South West) 155 in 1981

Built 1976
Number in Stock 1

455b NDF155P

467

Chassis Leyland Leopard PSU5C/4R
Bodywork Duple C51F
Ex-National Travel (South West) 167 in 1981

Built 1978
Number in Stock 1

467bh WFH167S

480/483

Chassis Leyland Leopard PSU3E/4R
Bodywork Plaxton C53F
Ex-National Travel (South West) 180/3 in 1981

Built 1978
Number in Stock 2

480ah WFH180S	**483**b AFH183T

484–498

Chassis Leyland Leopard PSU5C/4R
Bodywork Duple C50F (487: C32F, 498: C24F)
Ex-National Travel (South West) 184/7/9/90/5/8 in 1981

Built 1978/9
Number in Stock 6

484a AAD184S	**489**b AFH189T	**490**b AFH190T	**495**b AFH195T	**498**bh AFH198T
487ah AFH187T				

a Wessex fleetname   b Black & White fleetname   h National Holidays livery

WARRINGTON BOROUGH COUNCIL

The Corporation opened its first standard gauge electric tramway in April 1902, the final extension taking place in July 1905. Apart from the addition of six new cars in 1919 to the original 21, there were no further developments to the system.

Bus operation began in July 1913 with Tilling Stevens petrol electric double deckers and further vehicles of this make were purchased second hand. From 1924 Leylands of both single and double deck types were purchased, although two type 422 NSs and two six wheeled Renowns were purchased from AEC in 1928 and 1930.

The tramway system was converted to bus operation between 1931 and 1935 using Leyland Titans and Crossley Mancunians. There followed a period of expansion of the route network including some joint operations with Lancashire United Transport from 1938. In 1939 the Corporation acquired J.W. Pusill of Penketh, trading as "Suburban Motor Services" with seven vehicles of Leyland, Dennis and Bedford manufacture, including three Titans with rare Waveney double-deck bodywork. This mixture of types contrasted strongly with the almost complete standardisation on Leyland Titans after the tramway conversion, the only exception being a batch of Crossley Mancunians in 1936.

Apart from one "unfrozen" Leyland Titan delivered in 1942, no buses were added to stock during the war. However, one wartime development was the joint operation of a service with Naylor's Motor Services of Stockton Heath. This arrangement continued until December 1964 when the Corporation assumed the sole operation of the route.

Post-war vehicle policy was far from standardised, with Leyland Titans, Guy Arabs of both single and double deck types, Bristol K6Gs, and Foden PVD6s being supplied between 1946 and 1950. Between 1954 and 1956 the intake was eight Foden PVD6s and three Titans. From 1962 to 1965 a mixture of Leyland Titans and Daimler Fleetlines was placed in service, many of the former being only 7ft 6ins wide due to narrow streets in the town centre. Fleetlines continued to be purchased until 1973 but from 1967 until 1975 there was a rise in the proportion of single-deck vehicles, firstly in the form of Leyland Panther Cubs and from 1968 Bristol REs.

In 1973, the Corporation ventured into the coaching world with two Plaxton bodied Leopards, but in 1978 these were exchanged for three Derby City Transport Fleetlines. Leyland Titans were acquired from Leicester City Transport (PD3s) in 1975 and Brighton Corporation (PD2s) in 1978.

From 1977 to 1981 Leyland Atlanteans were purchased, joined in 1980 by ex London Transport DMS type Daimler Fleetlines. More recently Dennis Dominators and Leyland Olympians of 33-feet length have joined the fleet.

In April 1974 the joint routes with LUT were involved in a large scale regional reorganisation following the setting up of the Greater Manchester PTE and as a result LUT's share of operation passed to Crosville Motor Services. Joint operation of services with Crosville and North Western had been implemented in the late 1940s. Livery is red and white and buses are operated from a single garage in Wilderspool Causeway.

Warrington Borough Council Transport's fleet includes two 1972 East Lancashire dual purpose bodied Bristol RESL6Ls. No. 1 is seen here in the town centre. D.D. Kirk

From 1977 to 1981 the standard Warrington double deckers were Leyland Atlantean AN68s with East Lancashire bodies. No. 5 is an AN68A/1R supplied in 1978 D. Savage

During the decade between 1963 and 1973, the Daimler Fleetline CRG6LX with East Lancashire body was the standard double decker. No. 31 is one of the 1967 delivery and carries the final version of the East Lancashire body to have rounded domes. It retains the traditional fluted bar incorporating the Daimler name on the front panels. A.E. Hall

Illustrating the first of the later standard East Lancashire double deckers with peaked domes is 32, a 1970 Daimler Fleetline CRG6LX. It has since been withdrawn but it is still in stock at the time of writing. A.E. Hall

In 1978 Warrington exchanged two Leyland Leopard coaches with Derby City Transport and in return received three dual-doorway Roe bodied Daimler Fleetline CRG6LXs. They were new in 1970 and No. 40 (Derby 254) is seen in Warrington town centre. M.R. Keeley

Warrington is now pursuing a dual-sourcing policy in chassis purchase, both Dennis Dominators and Leyland Olympians being taken into stock. Delivered in 1982, No. 43 is one of the former and has an East Lancashire body seating no fewer than 88. The upper deck alone has a capacity of 51 which is similar to the total capacity of the average 'thirties or 'forties lowbridge double decker or a modern 11-metre single decker. D. Savage

Four East Lancashire dual-doorway bodied Bristol RESL6L buses were purchased in 1972, of which three survive. No. 61 is seen approaching the new bus station. R.L. Wilson

The front end treatment of eight similar vehicles delivered in 1975 was a little different, with the windscreen inset slightly and a plainer grille. No. 69, a Bristol RESL6L with East Lancashire dual-door bodywork is seen in Warrington. D. Savage

No. 81 is one of the Leyland Atlantean AN68s with East Lancashire bodies supplied to Warrington in 1977/8. D. Savage

Two Bristol-built Leyland Olympians (ONLXB/2R type) with East Lancashire bodies were purchased in 1982 following the Dominators by a couple of months. They have the same high seating capacity as the Dennises. D. Savage

Somewhat surprisingly, Warrington purchased six DMS class buses from London Transport in 1980. They all have Metro-Cammell Weymann bodywork rebuilt to single entrance and are based on Daimler Fleetline CRL6 chassis. Despite this designation, all have Gardner 6LX engines, these being fitted prior to entry into service with Warrington. No. 97 dates from 1973 and was formerly London Transport DMS1494. A.E. Hall

The final delivery of new Daimler Fleetline CRG6LXs, with East Lancashire bodies to Warrington arrived in 1973. Numerically the last, No. 105 is seen here in Warrington town centre. A.E. Hall

The oldest bus in public service in Warrington is 124, a 1963 Daimler Fleetline CRG6LX with East Lancashire body. Prior to 1981 it was numbered 24, in which guise it is seen in Horsemarket Street, Warrington. M.R. Keeley

WARRINGTON BOROUGH COUNCIL TRANSPORT FLEET LIST

1/2

Chassis Bristol RESL6L
Bodywork East Lancs DP40D
Built 1972
Number in Stock 2

1	YED274K	**2**w	YED275K

5–11

Chassis Leyland Atlantean AN68A/1R
Bodywork East Lancs H45/31F
Built 1978
Number in Stock 7

5	XTB5T	**7**	XTB7T	**9**	XTB9T	**10**	XTB10T	**11**	XTB11T
6	XTB6T	**8**	XTB8T						

12–17

Chassis Leyland Atlantean AN68A/1R (17: AN68B/1R)
Bodywork East Lancs H45/31F
Built 1980
Number in Stock 6

12	GEK12V	**14**	GEK14V	**15**	GEK15V	**16**	GEK16V	**17**	HED17V
13	GEK13V								

18–28

Chassis Leyland Atlantean AN68B/1R (23-28: AN68C/1R)
Bodywork East Lancs H45/31F
Built 1980/1
Number in Stock 11

18	MEK18W	**21**	MEK21W	**23**	MEK23W	**25**	OTB25W	**27**	OTB27W
19	MEK19W	**22**	MEK22W	**24**	OTB24W	**26**	OTB26W	**28**	OTB28W
20	MEK20W								

29–31

Chassis Daimler Fleetline CRG6LX
Bodywork East Lancs H45/32F
Built 1967
Number in Stock 3

29	HED856E	**30**	HED857E	**31**	HED858E

32–37

Chassis Daimler Fleetline CRG6LX
Bodywork East Lancs H43/29F
Built 1970
Number in Stock 2

32w	SED449H	**37**w	SED454H

38–40

Chassis Daimler Fleetline CRG6LX
Bodywork Roe H45/29D
Acquired from Derby City Transport (250/3/4) in 1978
Built 1970
Number in Stock 3

38	CRC250J	**39**	CRC253J	**40**	CRC254J

41–44

Chassis Dennis Dominator DDA156 (43/4: DDA159)
Bodywork East Lancs H51/37F
Built 1982
Number in Stock 4

41	CLV41X	**42**	CLV42X	**43**	CLV43X	**44**	CLV44X

48

Chassis Leyland Titan PD2/40 Special
Bodywork East Lancs H34/30F
Built 1965
Number in Stock 1

48t	BED729C

t Training bus

58–60

Chassis Bristol RESL6L
Bodywork Pennine B41D
Built 1970
Number in Stock 2

58w	UED574J	**60**w	UED576J

61–64

Chassis Bristol RESL6L
Bodywork East Lancs B40D

Built 1972
Number in Stock 3

61w YED269K **63**w YED271K **64**w YED272K

66–73

Chassis Bristol RESL6L
Bodywork East Lancs B41D (72:DP40F)

Built 1975
Number in Stock 8

66	JEK66N	**68**	JEK68N	**70**	LED70P	**72**	LED72P	**73**	LED73P
67	JEK67N	**69**	JEK69N	**71**	LED71P				

74–83

Chassis Leyland Atlantean AN68A/1R
Bodywork East Lancs H45/31F (75/7: H45/33F)

Built 1977/8
Number in Stock 10

74	TTB74S	**76**	TTB76S	**78**	TTB78S	**80**	TTB80S	**82**	TTB82S
75	REK75R	**77**	REK77R	**79**	TTB79S	**81**	TTB81S	**83**	TTB83S

84/85

Chassis Leyland (Bristol) Olympian ONLXB/2R
Bodywork East Lancs H51/37F

Built 1982
Number in Stock 2

84 CLV84X **85** CLV85X

94–99

Chassis Daimler Fleetline CRL6
Bodywork Metro-Cammell Weymann H44/27F
Ex-London Transport DMS1490/87/84/94, 1503/04 in 1980
Fitted with Gardner 6LX engines prior to acquisition

Built 1973
Number in Stock 6

94	MLH490L	**96**	MLH484L	**97**	MLH494L	**98**	THM503M	**99**	THM504M
95	MLH487L								

100–105

Chassis Daimler Fleetline CRG6LX
Bodywork East Lancs H43/29F

Built 1973
Number in Stock 6

100	NED351M	**102**	NED353M	**103**	NED354M	**104**	NED355M	**105**	NED356M
101	NED352M								

116

Chassis Leyland Titan PD2/40
Bodywork East Lancs H37/28R

Built 1964
Number in Stock 1

116t AED31B

t Training bus

124

Chassis Daimler Fleetline CRG6LX
Bodywork East Lancs H45/32F
Renumbered from 24 in 1981

Built 1963
Number in Stock 1

124 5833ED

Capital Transport

BOYLE STREET, CHEETHAM,
MANCHESTER, 8.

OPENING TIMES:— Beginning of April to the end of October. Wednesdays, Saturdays, Sundays and Bank Holidays. 10am–5pm.

ADMISSION:— Adults—40p.
Children (5–15) and OAPs—20p
Family Ticket £1.00.

HOW TO GET THERE:—The Museum is located one mile north of the city centre, close to the junction of Cheetham Hill Road (A665) and Queens Road (A6010).
Buses 35 and 59 from Piccadilly and Victoria.

The Museum of Transport is owned by Greater Manchester Transport and is operated on their behalf by volunteers of the Greater Manchester Transport Society. The collection of over fifty buses and service vehicles is drawn from the former transport operators of what is now the Greater Manchester County area and forms one of the largest and most colourful displays of its kind.

Part of the Museum's large collections of photographs, archive material and related items are also on display. The Museum is a working project and buses often attend rallies and local events. Other vehicles can be seen undergoing restoration work.

Between May and September the volunteers also operate a Vintage Bus Service in nearby Heaton Park using the Museum vehicles.

If you are interested in public transport in this area, why not join the Greater Manchester Transport Society? Send an s.a.e. to the Membership Secretary at the Museum address.

A MEMBER OF GREATER MANCHESTER'S TRANSPORT HERITAGE.

FLEET TOTALS AT 1.4.83

Chester	53
Double Deckers	
Leyland Fleetline FE30	18
Daimler Fleetline CRG	12
Dennis Dominator	11
Guy Arab	3
Single Deckers	
Leyland Leopard	9

Greater Manchester	2700
Double Deckers	
Leyland Atlantean AN68	1090
Daimler Fleetline CRG/L	606
Leyland Fleetline FE30	240
MCW Metrobus	170
Leyland Atlantean PDR2	111
Leyland Atlantean PDR1	36
Bristol VRT	25
Leyland Titan TN	15
Leyland Titan PD2	12
Scania Metropolitan	10
Leyland Titan PD3	5
Dennis Dominator	4
Volvo Ailsa	3
Leyland Olympian	2
Foden-NC	2
Single Deckers	
Leyland National	180
Leyland Leopard	86
Seddon IV	32
Bristol RESL	14
Seddon RU	13
Metro-Scania	13
Bristol RELL	8
AEC Reliance	6
Leyland Tiger	4
Bedford CF	4
Volvo B58	3
Ford Transit	2
Kassbohrer Setra	2
Leyland Panther	2

Halton	40
Double Deckers	
Leyland Titan PD2	1
Single Deckers	
Leyland National	17
Bristol RESL	8
Bristol RELL	7
Leyland Leopard	7

Merseyside	1259
Double Deckers	
Leyland Atlantean AN68	693
Leyland Atlantean PDR1	66
Bristol VRTSL	50
Scania Metropolitan	44
Daimler Fleetline CRG	40
Leyland Atlantean PDR2	40
Dennis Dominator	15
Leyland Olympian	15
MCW Metrobus	15
Leyland Titan PD2	5
Bristol VRTLH	4
Volvo Ailsa	2
Single Deckers	
Leyland National	180
AEC Swift	41
Metro-Scania	15
Bristol RESL	13
Leyland Tiger	12
Bristol LHS	4
Leyland Panther	2
Leyland Leopard	2
Leyland 550FG	1

National Travel (West)	267
Double Deckers	
Leyland Olympian	1
Single Deckers	
Leyland Leopard	249
Leyland Tiger	9
Bristol RELH	5
Dennis Falcon V	2
AEC Reliance	1

Warrington	78
Double Deckers	
Leyland Atlantean AN68	34
Daimler Fleetline CRG/L	21
Dennis Dominator	4
Leyland Olympian	2
Leyland Titan PD2	2
Single Deckers	
Bristol RESL	15